Boosting sales ... on a Shoestring

Increasing profits ... without breaking the bank

Bob Gorton

First published in Great Britain 2011 by A & C Black Publishers Ltd

This edition published 2011

Bloomsbury Publishing Plc

50 Bedford Square, London WC1B 3DP

British Library Cataloguing in Publication Data

A CIP record for this book is available from the British Library.

ISBN: 978-1-4081-3994-3

This book is produced using paper that is made from wood grown in managed, sustainable forests. It is natural, renewable and recyclable. The logging and manufacturing processes conform to the environmental regulations of the country of origin.

Design by Fiona Pike, Pike Design, Winchester

Typeset by RefineCatch Limited, Bungay, Suffolk

Printed and bound by CPI Group (UK) Ltd, Croydon, CR0 4YY

In memory of
Brian Warnes
The architect of the 'Value Added' technique

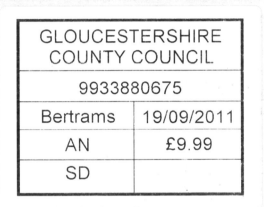

CONTENTS

ACKNOWLEDGEMENTS

Many of my business experiences are distilled in this book, both successes and the occasional disappointment. From each I have tried to understand what has happened (and why) and from that create for myself a set of rules that I have learned from them. It is these rules that I share with you.

Along the way, I've benefited from the advice offered by many generous people. Some of them were experienced business folk, some were amongst the world's best business writers and some were great academics writing several years ago; their conclusions are no less valid for that. They have given validity to my own half formed ideas, explained my own experiences and provided a foundation for my continuing interest, development and success. I've mentioned these resources for you throughout the book so that you can do your own further research if you want to.

I am also grateful to the many who have contributed to the information and observations included in this book:

- My family, on many counts — my wife Sue for her unfailing support in business, family and pleasure, my sons Alastair and Jeffrey for their discriminating support.
- Brian Warnes of Business Dynamics Ltd. for introducing me to the dynamics of business and the differential pricing concept.

INTRODUCTION

'It is true we do not have much money, so what we have to do is think.'

(Prof. Earnest Rutherford, who later split the atom)

My practical experience of starting and growing my own businesses has now extended into helping the many firms I now encounter and work with as a business advisor. These range from the one-man band turning over less than £100,000 and struggling to grow, through to the medium-sized enterprise which has annual sales of £25 million but fighting losses in a changing market. Despite the disparity of scale, the operators of these businesses all seem to face some combination of the same problems in their struggles to grow profitably:

1. **lack of cash**
2. **profit margins under pressure**
3. **not knowing where the next order is coming from**

These are the focus of my attention for this book. Margins, sales and cash, are the killers or winners, the prime levers by which every business either dies or flourishes. I link these with another critical area that is frequently overlooked: which is, the productive capacity of a business to deliver whatever is being sold by it.

Once a business has correctly understood its competitive position, it is the linking of sales demand, profitability and resource capacity which provides the key for stable, profitable growth. Getting this connection right is what powerfully uplifts the profitability of a business, which generates the cash needed to expand and grow further and commits the sales and production teams to the same agenda.

Small businesses

What is a small business? There are various definitions depending on purpose – for example, the rules for bankers and accounts filing tend to be based on turnover[1] – but the most useful and commonly used definitions are based on the number of people a company employs:

- **0–9 employees = micro business**
- **10–49 employees = small firm**
- **50–249 employees = medium-sized enterprise**

Collectively, this group is called SMEs (small and medium-sized enterprises). However, there is an argument that the medium-sized enterprises should be regarded differently from the small and micro companies because they have very different operating characteristics.[2] Although the rules of successful business growth are the same whatever the size of the firm, it is the smaller-sized companies that are more vulnerable to the slings and arrows of outrageous business fortune.

Micro and small firms are hugely important for the economy of any country and they collect and pay tax, National Insurance contributions, Value Added Tax and other dues which help pay for all the public services the population enjoys. Check out these statistics for the UK:[3]

- **In 2008, there were 4.8 million private sector enterprises in the UK.**
- **Only 0.1% of these are large firms with 250 or more employees, employing 40.6% of the working population of 23.1 million people**

- The other 99.9% are SMEs employing the other 59.4%. Of these:

	% Enterprises	% Employees
Those with no employees (only self employed managers	74.1%	16.8%
Micro businesses (1–9 employees)	21.6%	16.7%
Small firms (10–49 employees)	3.6%	14.4%
Medium-sized enterprise (50–249 employees)	0.6%	11.5%

Significantly, 95.7% of all UK enterprises employ less than 10 people but provide employment for 33.5% of the workforce: nearly 8 million people. Taken together with the small firms, this group is the backbone of the UK economy accounting for over £1 billion (36.5%) of private sector turnover and 64% of all commercial innovations.

Over 500,000 people start up their own business every year. Regrettably, the survival rates for businesses that have registered for VAT indicate that many of us who make the attempt to set up in business quickly discover how hard it really is in practice. Of all new businesses that register for VAT only 92% survive their first year and 29% fail within three years.[4] The actual figure, including those that do not register for VAT, is probably much higher.

This simple statement illustrates that if starting a business isn't risky enough, growing it – which is what survival means in the business world – is even more hazardous. In almost every other field of endeavour, the wastage from such failure rates would be unacceptable and these ratios have only marginally improved since 1995.

INTRODUCTION

Businesses that are involved in the provision of services have the worst one-year survival rate of all. This is a worry, because services account for around 70% of the gross domestic product in developed countries[5] and companies in industries that have high value orders and customers that call the shots are at notoriously high risk of having their businesses swept away on a tide of low margins and increasing cash-flow difficulties. These can suddenly become catastrophic if a single customer plays a 'take it or leave it card' or delays payment. Such risks are multiplied many times in those industries where design or new technology is a component of the supply, leaving the scope for argument much wider.

This book

What is needed is something that links two things:

1. **a recognition of the underlying relationships between growth, risk and profitability that impact on the imperative for a business to grow**
2. **practical techniques that will deliver that growth in a low-risk, affordable way**

This book has been written with these issues in mind and will fundamentally shift the odds of success in your favour by describing proven methods for growing a business on a shoestring budget in a safe and stable way.

The greatest potential for benefit will be amongst those owners and operators of small firms operating in the business-to-business arena, either producing items for sale or providing services. The book will also be particularly helpful to those companies operating in a technical arena or where the business has a relatively small number of high value customers.

My approach is to take a systematic look at the underlying mechanisms for the success of a business before suggesting tactics for boosting sales. This is because, if money is tight, we can't afford to make expensive mistakes or to simply throw money at a technique in the hope that it will work!

Numbers

Countless business managers have discovered, often the hard way, that what gets measured, gets done and what *isn't* being measured is either not happening at all or dangerously out of control. Quantifying the effect and outcomes of the approaches described is absolutely crucial to growing a business safely and doing the right things to make it grow. How else will you discover what works and what doesn't?

I sympathise with those of you whose minds go blank at the thought of reams of numbers on the page. Having said that, bear with me: the plain fact is that linking your business reality to the underlying laws of what makes profit and how to calculate it is at the very heart of creating business success.

So I've included numbers and worked examples in the book to illustrate and support what I'm saying. Skip over them if you wish but I urge you to look at them. If it helps to make things less abstract, think of putting in the effort to understand the 'sums', as making the difference between having your new Mercedes or your creditors' Administrative Receivers turning up in the car park. It's true, believe me – I've had both!

Customers

When I set up my first business I remember being incredibly confused about all the things there were to do. I really wanted to get it right and everybody had their own opinions on what was most important. I had to think about company registration, VAT registration, a bank, and then there was the accounts system, premises, health and safety, staff legislation, quality management ... the list seemed endless.

Then a business colleague visited me from the United States and said: 'I can see you're doing a great job, Bob, but have you found any customers yet? Because without someone who wants to buy what you're offering, none of this needs to exist!'

He was right. There is so much advice available on how to set up a business and operate it, that it can be easy to forget the most important thing:

'It is a customer who determines what a business is. It is the customer alone whose willingness to pay for a good or service converts economic resources into wealth and things into goods ... What the customer thinks he/she is buying, what he/she considers value, is decisive – the customer is the foundation of a business and keeps it in existence.'[6]

If you keep this in mind, you'll be successful.

Have fun with this book. It's going to improve your business no end.

Notes/References

1. Companies House, (2005). *CHN19 Disclosure Requirements*. www. companieshouse. co.uk.
2. Leach, P. & Birn, R. (2005). *Taking the M out of SME*, BDO Stoy Hayward & The Institute of Chartered Accountants in England & Wales (June).
3. Department for Business Innovations & Skills (2009). *Statistical Press Release URN 09/92.*

4. DTI Small Business Service Analytical Unit (2007), *Survival rates of VAT registered enterprises, 1995–2004 key results* www.sbs.gov.uk/survival *URN 07/963.*

5. Ruskin-Brown, I. (1996). *Marketing Your Service Business*, Thorogood.

6. Drucker, P. F. (1973). *Management: Tasks, Responsibilities and Practices*, Harper Row.

1 ARE YOU *SURE* YOU WANT TO BOOST SALES?

In the beginning, a business starts out with a customer or two and then wins a few more by doing what works well at the time. But time passes, and the business gets comfortable. Often, looking out for new customers and opportunities falls by the wayside. If you've found yourself saying any of the following statements, you'll recognise the pattern:

- The things we did before always brought in enough customers, so why should we change?
- We tried some promotional things but they never worked. We were wasting money so we stopped doing it.
- We don't know anyone who can help us increase sales effectively.
- We had a marketing budget but when times got hard we cut it to save the money.
- We are afraid of growing too fast and not being able to cope with the extra business.

If you don't look for new leads (often called *prospects*) continuously, it's likely that your business will end up in a 'feast or famine' cycle:

you either have no work at all or so much that you can't keep on top of it. Eventually, though, your business will become overly dependent on a small number of customers. Then margins start to get crushed because the few customers you have are critically important to your business, so when they ask for lower prices it is hard to refuse. The other problem is that no buyer stays around for ever; even loyal customers move on to other suppliers for any number of reasons (none of which you can control), and they leave a void when they go. When times get hard in your market, as they surely will from time to time, a crisis point is reached when something has to be done but by then there is no money left in the pot to do it with.

You're presumably reading this book because you feel the need to grow sales but don't have a lot of cash to invest in that activity. This is most likely because the above is horribly familiar. It's probable that:

- **you're running an established business that needs more sales, but not generating sufficient profit to fund the process and can't get the money to do it from elsewhere.**
- **you're operating a new, or relatively new, business with hardly any spare money. You're not alone, though: nearly all young businesses have this problem!**
- **you're cautious about investing funds and don't believe that money spent on marketing activity is guaranteed to deliver results, so you resent spending it because it's all a bit of a gamble.**

Sound familiar?

Do you want to boost sales on a shoestring? If the answer is yes, then this book is for you. Except that the title is misleading. It should really be called *Boosting Profitability . . . on a Shoestring*. Why? Because improving *profit* is what this is really all about; increasing the *right sort* of sales is simply one mechanism for achieving profitable growth.

Warning signs

When you're planning to boost sales there are many potential traps to look out for, hence our focus on improving profitability as an integral part of growing sales. It's much safer. Many a business has gone bust whilst increasing sales turnover and it's a fact that fast-growth businesses are more prone to failure.[1]

I believe that rapidly increasing sales is the second most dangerous thing a business can do (after not selling enough!).

Profits slump and overheads hump

Small businesses are particularly vulnerable because they are usually short of important resources like cash. But draw comfort from the fact that the very high risks of rapid sales growth can affect big businesses as well as smaller ones.

For example, in the 1980s, the luxury leather brand, Gucci, set out to grow revenue aggressively on the back of its prestigious name by adding lower-priced canvas products to its range. It pushed products into department stores and duty-free channels while simultaneously licensing its name to appear on a range of items like watches, sunglasses and perfumes.

Gucci's revenue soared but sales of its most expensive and lucrative products fell away, leading to a dramatic fall in overall profitability. Gucci recovered but had alienated its most profitable customers and attracted a larger but much less attractive mix of customers from the profitability point of view.[2]

The Gucci lesson highlights an important problem with boosting sales: the strategies that many businesses have adopted to grow revenue have actually eroded profit margins and reduced the bottom line – in other words, they're selling more but making much less money!

Gross profit

Gross profit is the money you have left over once you have sold your goods or services and you've paid for the cost of providing or creating them. It's critically important because it's used to pay for the costs of running the business – the overheads – and what's left can be used to help the business grow. The 'overheads' include things such as the rent, heat, light, marketing and so on. Gross profit is so important because if you don't earn enough of it, then you can't pay these bills – it's as simple as that. Once the overheads have been paid for, anything left is called *net profit*. Net profit is what you're after, because once you've given Her Majesty's Revenue and Customs their share, you can give some to the shareholders, save it or spend it on anything you like.

Many business operators today focus on boosting revenues, believing that increased sales will bring more profits. This assumption is deeply flawed unless maintaining *gross margin percentage* is an integral part of the plan. Gross margin percentage is the gross profit divided by the £ value of sales and it is frequently used to indicate how effective a business is at making money from what it does.

Gross *margin* is the percentage of gross profit related to the amount of sales. So if you sold something for £100 and it cost £70 to produce:

- **the gross profit is £30 (£100 LESS £70)**
- **the gross margin is 30% (£30 DIVIDED BY £100)**

It's easy to visualise what happens if sales are doubled but the gross margin percentage is halved in the process: the amount of profit will remain the same. If, simultaneously, overheads have increased to handle the growth in trade (more administrative staff, bigger buildings, larger fleet of vehicles and so on) then the outcome can be a *fall* in overall net profitability.

The result is a dis-economy of scale, which can easily happen if things are not very carefully managed. The little outfit that was profitably operating with 8–9 people could comfortably assume that everyone knew what they were doing and that they talked to each other frequently to get the job done as efficiently as possible. If there was ever a glitch in the system, everyone knew about it, including the owner. Once an organisation employs over 50 people, though, you can't get them all in the same room! So you have to divert time to meetings, training and other related activities that keep everyone on track. In other words, a proportion of staff time is spent managing people rather than directly doing the things that make money for the business. This adds to the costs without adding anything to the bottom line, which is one characteristic that makes running a medium-sized enterprise very different to running a small or micro one.

The dangers of growth are:

- **profits do not follow revenues. It's perfectly possible for profits to fall when revenues increase and this frequently happens by accident. Scary but true!**
- **overheads don't rise in a linear fashion. There are 'step' changes that can be dangerously out of kilter with the contribution from profits that need to be earned to pay for them. These might occur when the increase in trade just reaches that critical mass when another expensive machine is required, or forces a move into bigger premises.**

Turbulence is inevitable

Before embarking on a journey towards growth, you really do need to pack your stress pills. The traumas associated with building a business and handling the burden of an increasingly complex organisation are well documented.

As long ago as 1972, Greiner[3] (then Associate Professor of Organisational Behaviour at Harvard Business School) argued that growing organisations move through five relatively calm periods of evolution, each of which ends with a *period of crisis and revolution*.

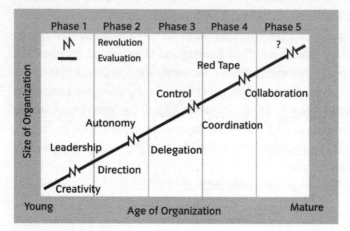

Figure 1.1[4]

Subsequently in 1983, Churchill and Lewis[5] told us they had identified five stages of business growth, each of which was characterised by a different type of crisis, including one they couldn't pinpoint:

1. *Crisis* of leadership
2. *Crisis* of autonomy

3. *Crisis* of control
4. *Crisis* of red tape
5. *Crisis* of something else undefined

So not much comfort there, then!

In 1988, Ichak Adizes[6] described ten stages of corporate life cycle as a basis for understanding how to improve the performance of business and government and emphasised the need to make 'fundamental changes without the **chaos and destructive conflict** that plague many efforts'.

Scarier still . . . (See Figure 1.2.)

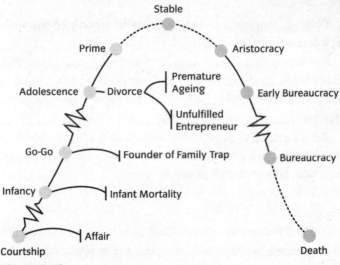

Figure 1.2[7]

Then, as if that wasn't enough, BDO Stoy Hayward, a leading firm of chartered accountants, published their 'Diamond Growth Model'[8] that compared academic viewpoints with the real-life experiences of their customers. At each stage of business growth,

• Cash-flow pressures	• Over-promise/under-deliver
• Difficulty in attracting good staff	• People and concept burnout
• IT strategy	• Loss of flexibility
• Skill deficiencies	• Lack of corporate expertise
• Strained communications	• Dampened innovation
• Changing culture	• Nobody 'owns' the business
• Loss of entrepreneurial spirit	• Bureaucracy
• Management surpasses leadership	• Ivory towers
	• Need to de-layer
• Loss of executive motivation	• Stretching the brand

Figure 1.3

they identified damaging issues, which included those listed in Figure 1.3.

Chillingly, they conclude that '**successful growth brings with it a loss of control**'.

The highlighting in each case is mine. I want to illustrate that many bright, intelligent people have been working on the problems associated with growing businesses for years. These problems are real.

But we are not alone and, thankfully, there is a lot we can do to combat them using techniques that have been proven by people who have been through it all before.

Cash: The big pitfall

Right, so if you're setting out to boost sales, you have to recognise that growth is hazardous and that you have to avoid, at all costs, the primary causes of small business failure: chaos; conflict; loss of control; and running out of cash.

Whatever the reason behind it (and there can be many good ones), a lack of ready cash will kill the business every time.

The fact that you're contemplating 'shoestring' tactics implies that you don't have much cash in the first place. This makes you particularly vulnerable because it's much more likely that you'll run out of it quickly. As we noted above, many small and medium-sized businesses complain that they're under-financed. This is mainly because most firms don't have enough security to borrow the money they need, and also because small and medium-sized firms are inherently riskier than bigger concerns, which means that shareholders are less likely to invest in them.

Obviously if a business is losing money, cash will be running out. Cash gaps can also be caused by poor credit control and lack of planning, especially if profit margins are thin. These problems have to be fixed before a business even thinks about growing. But few people realise that even *profitable* companies can run out of cash if they try to grow too quickly – a growing business requires more cash for working capital than one that isn't.

Working capital

Cash runs out of a growing business quickly because generating more sales means that you need more 'working capital'. Working capital is the amount of money it takes to bridge the gap between when you have to pay for something to be produced and when you can collect the customer's money. It is crucial to any business.

If an increase in sales is achieved at the expense of profit – that is, by reducing prices but not cutting manufacturing or creation costs to compensate – then, taken together, the effects of the reduction in profit and increased turnover multiply to dramatically increase the cash needed to fund the business in the short term. If the growth continues to be driven by lower profits for any length of time, the consequence of the ongoing cash drain can be catastrophic and permanent.

If a company is underwritten by a deep treasure chest, like Gucci, this classic mistake may be survivable. Otherwise it explains why so many growing businesses outgrow their overdraft facility, or end up with a constant debt rather than a fluctuating one – which is what it was designed to be.

When there's continuing increasing pressure on bank borrowings as a result of growth, the smallest shift in your banker's confidence – which might be the result of something you did, or something external, such as a change in the bank's policy, or a tragedy like 9/11 – can make them want to press the panic button, at which point they will, at best, clamp down on borrowing or, at worst, call in the loan. When the money runs out and financial support is withdrawn, the business fails. It is as simple as that.

You will see how to minimise the chances of that happening to your business in chapter 2.

Why risk it?

If growing your business means threatening profitability, increasing overheads, turbulence, loss of control and umpteen other crisis points, all topped off with a very high probability of running out of cash, why would you bother? Indeed, you could ask yourself why nearly everyone you speak to is encouraging you to do it.

And it's a good question to ask. All sorts of people and organisations will encourage you to grow for a variety of reasons:

- **bankers want you to grow the business because this will increase the demand for cash resources (such as loans or overdrafts). They will profit by lending money to you.**
- **accountants want you to grow the business because it increases demand for their services, especially tax planning, sorting you out when things go wrong and**

eventually selling your business when things go right,
which is where the big bucks are.

■ the government wants you to grow the business
because it increases demand for employment and
contributes to the Treasury.

The point is that all these agencies have their own agenda but
there is one constant: the very high risks of growth are always left
with the owners who stand to lose their job, lifestyle, investment,
heritage and legacy if things go 'pear-shaped'. This is of course, as
it should be, because the shareholders bear the lion's share of
reward along with all the risk.

So why do owners want to take on increased risk in exchange for
growth, especially since the chances of failure seem heavily weighted
against them?

Frankly, some don't. The vast majority of businesses in the UK in
2008 were firms that didn't employ anyone (74.1%)[9] and many had
no pretensions to growth. Their owners are content just to earn a
living that maintains their lifestyle; unsurprisingly, these are known
as 'lifestyle businesses'. Some business owners have inherited their
company and just want to preserve the heritage. Their motivation is
often very different from those entrepreneurs who start them up or
buy them.

Lifestyle preferences aside, if you're not actively growing your
business, it's not standing still and not necessarily safe either. Why?
Because every other business is growing around you. Lack of growth
means relative regression, which will eventually become
overwhelming – the faster growing grass in your field of endeavour
will take all the sunlight.

In the opposite camp are those people who disregard the risks
and get carried away with a 'gung-ho' attitude that ignores potential

pitfalls. Rarely is this due to greed; more often it is a combination of well-intentioned enthusiasm and an excitable personality. This type of entrepreneurial attitude is frequently encouraged by those who will profit from it, but who don't share the risk and don't actually put in any hands-on work to make it happen. Which is fine for all concerned if it works out, but do you really want that level of uncontrolled risk in your business? I wouldn't. I hold to the maxim:

Turnover is vanity, profit is sanity and cash is the reality

Growth is essential to survival. For the owners of a small or medium-sized business, a *managed approach to growth* can provide a degree of security and wealth that would be unimaginable in any sort of employment. This is what we are aiming to achieve, ultimately: you're trying to build a sustainable profitable enterprise that doesn't require the full-time attention of the owner.

Provided we can accomplish that honestly and ethically then everything else we aspire to in terms of giving something back to the society that helped us get there, can be better achieved once those objectives are attained.

What about the rest of the team?

You need to think about the possible consequences of growing sales on the other stakeholders in the business. Growth has an impact on every single part of an organisation and affects everyone involved with it. It's still risky even when it's modified by a managed approach to cash and profitability. Before you embark on your campaign, you need to be absolutely sure that a growth strategy is right for you, your business and the other people involved. Think carefully about the risks, time, effort and money involved and ask yourself:

ARE YOU *SURE* YOU WANT TO BOOST SALES?

- What will I gain?
- What might I lose?
- Is it all worth it?

- What will others gain?
- What might they lose?
- Is it worth it for them?

The process of arriving at a consensus on the way forward is sometimes called a 'stakeholder review'. It requires you to do some thinking and have some conversations with key colleagues.

Here are some questions that may be helpful in provoking your thoughts:

1. **Why do you personally want to boost sales?**

   - **Where was the business meant to be going originally?**
   - **Why did it seem like a good idea at the time?**
   - **Where do you want to take the business after all?**
   - **What are your personal goals and aspirations and those of your family?**
   - **Have you thought about your work-life balance and the impact that a growth strategy will have upon it and those closest to you?**
   - **What do you want from the business as the final outcome?**

2. **Make a list of the primary stakeholders such as partners, family, fellow directors and so on, and note their reasons for being involved with the business.**

   - **What are *their* future objectives?**
   - **What do they want for the business?**
   - **What do they want from the business?**

3. **List the reasons why boosting sales would be good for each of the primary stakeholders in your business as honestly and accurately as you can.**
4. **What are the requirements and objectives of the secondary stakeholders? These might include:**

- Accountant
- Bank
- Customers (top 20%)
- Employees
- Investors
- Landlord
- Lenders
- Suppliers

5. **Do you have other secondary stakeholders who may be affected? Will they be supportive? Concerned? Negative?**

Don't be surprised if not everyone shares your aspirations. You can, of course, address others' concerns by listening and talking to them, but you may just have to accept that some people involved with business aren't as ambitious as you, may be upset by change and won't be comfortable with the turbulence that will be caused by growth. If you think of your business like a bus travelling on a long journey: not all the people who joined it whilst travelling the 'leafy lanes' will be as comfortable on board when it is travelling at full speed around an inner-city ring road.

A senior level financial manager once remarked to me: 'I only chose this career because it was indoor work with no heavy lifting and I can go home every day at 5 o'clock'. This type of personality is unlikely to cope well with the turmoil that will erupt when you start pushing the sales through the roof. If you're the boss, you'll have to manage reactions like this. You'll also have to accept that if you are determined to start aggressively growing the business, some people may choose to leave. This is painful, especially if you've been working with those people for some time, but it's also healthy. You'll need everyone to be fully on-board and supportive as your plans take shape.

The one-page business plan

OK, so you've thought carefully about your own aspirations as well as those of other key shareholders. If everyone else who matters is on-board and you're still ready to go for it, it's time to start pinning down details and objectives so that you have a framework to work with. Preparing a short statement of what you intend to do can be a useful way of focusing on future activities. What is needed is something crisp and to the point that can act as a guiding star when all other sense of direction is lost. A one-page business plan[10] is the ideal tool for crystallising the vision for everyone involved in the business (it's very different from the 'vision' and 'mission' statements that you may have heard about, and much more useful because the objectives are quantified).

These are useful questions for clarifying that vision:

■ **Where are you going? Only you can answer this question by defining what your aspirations are. Make sure that your answer is positively phrased, specific, and quantifiable in terms of time and money.**
■ **How are you going to get there? This book should provide most of the answers.**
■ **When will you know you have arrived? Again, you'll need to be specific. What will you see, hear and feel? What will others see, hear and feel?**

Ideally a one-page business plan should have four sections:[11]

1. the unique business proposition that defines who you are as a company in positive terms
2. the purpose, which identifies your customers and how you serve them
3. the goals, including the overall objective and one or two key stepping stones
4. the strategy that explains how the business is going to achieve its goals

For example:

> Rock and Tile is the number one UK trade supplier/installer of BOTH natural stone and manufactured tile products.
>
> We add value to building contractors through our single-source offering and by providing ZERO-DEFECT installations that minimise time, cost and management risks.
>
> Rock and Tile's immediate goal is to grow to £6m in annual net sales at 25% gross margin over three years. This is so that a management team can be cultivated to deliver stakeholder value without the full-time management control of the shareholders.
>
> The plan is to:
>
> ■ increase sales performance by using marketing processes. This will grow turnover at least 20% annually whilst maintaining or improving gross margin through greater penetration of the fit-out market segment.

- at the same time, we shall positively attract more customers and increase existing customer loyalty by consistently delivering high-quality service. This will result in Rock and Tile being specified more frequently as the preferred supplier/installer, thus increasing the proportion of directly negotiated and repeat orders and reducing dependence on competitive tendering.

The result of increasing the loyal customer base and enhancing the reputation of the business will maximise our influence in the industry and improve profitability. Where appropriate, we shall also seek to accelerate this growth and achieve diversification by relevant acquisitions.

Growing a stable, profitable business in this way will minimise commercial risk and enhancing the reputation of the firm. Subsequently, this will allow strong branding to be used as a vehicle to promote and expand the business throughout the UK.

Having thought about the implications, and rallied the rest of the team around a common objective, expressed by the one-page business plan: if you're still ready to go for it, let's move on and look at 'safe' ways to grow and how to manage the risks that come with it.

Notes/References

1. Cressey, R. (1999). Centre for Small and Medium Sized Enterprises at Warwick Business School.
2. Gadiesh, O. & Gilbert, J. L. (1998). 'Profit pools: a fresh look at strategy.' *Harvard Business Review*, May-Jun.

3. Greiner, L. E. (1972). 'Evolution and revolution as organizations grow.' *Harvard Business Review*, Jul–Aug, pp. 37–46.
4. *http://www.accel-team.com*
5. Churchill, N, C. & Lewis, V. L. (1983). 'The five stages of small business growth.' *Harvard Business Review*, May–Jun, pp. 30–50.
6. Adizes, I (1988). *Corporate Lifecycles: How Organizations Grow and Die and What to Do About It.* www.adizes.com.
7. www.adizes.com
8. Baines, A. & Sinhal, R. (1999). *Business Grow How: The Stepping Stones to Successful Growth*, BDO Stoy Hayward Accountancy Books.
9. Department for Business Innovation & Skills (2009), *Statistical Press Release URN 09/92.*
10. Horan. J. (1998). *The One Page Business Plan*, The One Page Business Plan Company.
11. Kramers, K. (2001). *CEO Tools: The Nuts and Bolts of Business for Every Manager's Success*, Gandy Dancer Press.

2 THE 'ONE NUMBER' WAY TO TRANSFORM YOUR BUSINESS

Good preparation is an essential part of growing your business safely. After all, you wouldn't set out on a motoring journey across Europe without making sure that your car was up to it, would you? And if your car was a bit the worse for wear, it would be a good idea to arrange the route so you avoided the fastest roads, the biggest mountains and planned some frequent stops to check up on things, wouldn't it?

As previously mentioned, it is vitally important to boost profitability before embarking on any sales growth programme. Otherwise there is a real danger that low margin sales growth will strip cash out of the business faster than the rate at which it is being earned, resulting in failure of the business through what is called 'Over Trading'.

The safe way to grow a business is to use this 'One Number' approach, which will improve profitability and cash flow: then sales growth can be driven safely. It often happens inevitably as a by-product of the technique because understanding the 'One Number' enables prices to be matched to customer's appetite for what the business can do for them.

The 'One Number' approach recognises that there is a limitation that will inhibit growth in every type of business. Correctly identifying this 'Critical Resource Limitation', and designing the business around it, can be the key to dramatically improving profitability whilst reducing pressure on resources and then allowing sales to be improved.

The concept connects the Critical Resource Limitation to the financial drivers of a business through the Break-even Point: which is the turnover figure that will give a profit that exactly balances the overhead expenditure.

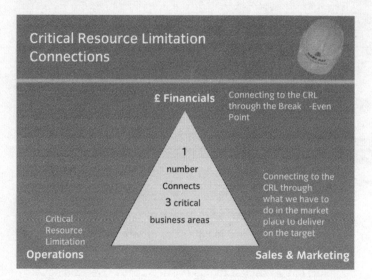

Understanding the value that must be added to the Break-even Point for selling the company's resources results in the 'One Number' target that will deliver the planned profitability. This informs sales and marketing by highlighting those product and customer combinations that will maximise the value added from sales and operational constraints.

Price flexing to win deals that give the best possible return for the business resources always results in a rapid and dramatic improvement in profitability whilst simultaneously 'relaxing' operations and releasing them from the 'Busy Fools' treadmill.

The technique has never failed to increase the bottom line profitability and sales of any business where it has been correctly applied.

Let's explore how it is applied.

To use the 'One Number' technique you also to be fully on top of the following factors:

- the *Break-even Point*, which is an expression of the current trading condition of the business. In particular, the balance of turnover, profitability and running expenses.
- the *Critical Resource Limitation*, which is the limiting factor of the resources used by trading. How do they hold back growth?
- the range of *Value Added for the Critical Resource Limitation*, which is how you will maximise the value you can add to balance sales and resources for maximum profitability
- the *Safe Rate of Growth*. How much cash is available? We're working on the assumption that there wasn't much there to start off with, but what is being generated from trading? What is the Self Financing Growth Rate, which is the maximum rate at which it is safe to grow before the cash supply becomes threatened?

Only after we have clearly understood the *capacity* of the business to grow should we consider the mechanisms that will make that growth happen.

Let's look at each of these issues in turn.

Break-even Point

The point at which the level of sales of goods and services results in profits that exactly cover the operating expenses of the company is called the *Break-even Point*. This figure is one of the most effective and important financial ratios for indicating the trading health of a business.[1] Yet for some reason, it seldom appears high on those 'classic' schedules of key performance indicators that accountants and analysts use.

The Break-even Point is an expression of the current condition of a business. It is a very powerful indicator of the strategies that should be pursued for growth. For that, you'll need to know the *gross margin percentage* of your business, which is the proportion of gross profit in relation to sales turnover.

A business turning over £1.2 million at 25% gross margin and £240,000 overheads is much healthier than a business turning over £3.6 million at 21% gross margin with £720,000 overheads (which is proportionally the same). The former is making £60,000, which is respectable for a business that size, but the latter only £36,000, which is tiny in proportion to the sales!

Look at these two examples of trading accounts for Smith and Jones:

	Smith Ltd	**Jones Ltd**
Sales	£ 1,200,000	£ 3,600,000
Cost of sales	£ 900,000	£ 2,844,000
Gross profit	£ 300,000 25%	£ 756,000 21%
Overheads	£ 240,000	£ 720,000
Net profit	£ 60,000	£ 36,000

The risks in Jones Ltd, the £3.6 million business with £36k net profit, are much higher for three reasons:

1. **a relatively small shift in the market causing a 1% reduction in gross margin will leave the £3 million business with zero net profit (close to losing money), but the £1 million business will still make £48,000.**
2. **overheads are difficult to reduce quickly in troubled times because they usually consist of long-term commitments such as rent or staff costs that are hard to 'turn off' at low cost.**
3. **overheads do not rise in a linear fashion; there are incremental changes such as the move to larger premises or the acquisition of a new machine that can create a surge of costs that threaten to overwhelm the business from time to time.**

Not understanding these immutable facts will nearly always lead to a crash; it's a bit like not understanding why a speed limit is important!

The relationship between turnover, gross margin and overheads is the essence of understanding the importance of the *Break-even Point*.

It is so effective as an indicator of business health because the calculation uses all of the components that affect profitability and ultimately cash, which is the life-blood of the business:

- **sales volume (turnover)**
- **cost of sales**
- **administrative expenses (overheads)**

With these three numbers, taken from the company accounts, we can form a view of trading health for the business that will be an important guide to where we should focus our selling activities. Here is how the Break-even Point, and its relationship to the actual turnover of a business, is calculated:

a) Gross profit $=$ Turnover $-$ Cost of sales

b) Gross margin % $= \dfrac{\text{Gross profit}}{\text{Turnover}}$

c) Break-even turnover $= \dfrac{\text{Overhead}}{\text{Gross margin \%}}$

d) Break-even turnover % $= \dfrac{\text{Break-even turnover}}{\text{Turnover}}$

Figure 2.1

a) Illustrates how the *gross profit* is calculated.
b) Illustrates how the *gross margin %* is calculated.
c) *Break-even turnover* is the break-even point for the business. It is the amount of sales volume at the established gross margin % that will enable the business to just cover its overhead expenses.
d) *Break-even turnover %* gives the relationship between the actual turnover and the break-even turnover.

The implications of *break-even turnover %* for trading health can be seen as follows:

Trading health

	>95% 'suicidal'	Certain to fail if uncorrected
Ratio of actual	90%–95% Dangerous	Likely to go bust at first misfortune
turnover to break-even turnover	80%–90% Risky but manageable	Probably seeing periodic cash pressure
	70%–80% Acceptable	Sustain or improve
	60%–70% Strong	Safe
	<60% Exceptionally good	Generating adequate cash for growth and dividends

Figure 2.2

Let's see how this applies to the companies we were looking at earlier:

	Smith Ltd	Jones Ltd
Turnover	£1,200,000	£3,600,000
Cost of sales	£900,000	£2,844,000
Gross profit	£300,000	£756,000
Gross margin %	25.0%	21.0%
Overheads	£240,000	£720,000
Break-even turnover	£960,000	£3,428,571
Break-even turnover %	80.0%	95.2%

Figure 2.3

The implications for this on growth strategy are clear:

- Smith Ltd is probably OK. They should work towards boosting sales volume, or turnover, while taking care to maintain or improve the gross margin % at or above 25%.

- Jones Ltd is already 'Suicidal', and attempting to boost sales volume would increase the trading risk. Even a tiny disturbance in gross margin is likely to result in the company making a loss. Any boosting strategy should focus on improving the gross margin % *before* increasing sales volume. Doing it the other way round will not only increase the risk of losses, but is also probably going to cause a cash-flow crisis: the increased demand for working capital is unlikely to be sustained by the cash generated from the current level of profitability.

Because growing turnover for Jones Ltd would be so risky, it's best not to even think about going there. Instead, Jones Ltd should concentrate on improving profitability, even if this has to be achieved at the expense of sales. It is perfectly possible for profits to increase when revenues are constant or falling; when this happens it is usually by careful management. This is often the main strategy in business recovery and turnaround situations because, when carefully managed, it improves cash flows.

The design benchmark break-even/turnover relationship for a secure, profitable, well-funded business is <75%. How does your company fare?

Now, using the example above, work out the *break-even turnover* % for your own business and decide what your booster strategy should be, based on the following:

- **More than 90% – boost gross margin % and reduce overheads**
- **80% to 90% – boost gross margin % *then* boost turnover**

■ **Less than 80% – boost turnover while preserving or improving gross margin %**

Critical Resource Limitation

Every business has at least one important factor that limits the amount of trade it can undertake and which might constrain the growth or amount of money that can be made. This is called the *Critical Resource Limitation*. Identifying your firm's *Critical Resource Limitation* correctly is essential if you want to avoid 'overheating' the business by selling too much of something you're going to run out of.

But surely if we can just get more business everything will sort itself out, won't it?

Wrong.

The techniques for growth described later in this book will work – often dramatically well. As a result, you'll need to make sure that your business isn't overwhelmed with success. Although that sounds like a nice problem to have, it is another reason why growing quickly is so dangerous if you're not prepared, because accepting orders you can't fulfil is very damaging. Taking on too much work, or overselling your capacity will:

■ **create demand you cannot satisfy – the competition then scoops up your dissatisfied customers**
■ **have a negative impact on quality as you struggle to cope**
■ **eat up money as you get in stock for orders you then can't complete and collect the cash for**
■ **waste money on promotional resources generating new customers you can't satisfy**

Furthermore, planning your selling activities around your capacity to produce is one way to maximise profits.

Think carefully about what the Critical Resource Limitation is in your business, because it may not be what your first instinct suggests. Most people, when asked what is holding their business back, will reply 'cash', 'lack of customers', 'the sales team', 'the competition' or whatever is causing them angst at the time. But these are not in themselves *Critical Resource Limitations* because, although problematic, they can usually be worked around and are not, therefore, fundamental constraints that will inhibit growth.

Here are some examples of potential *Critical Resource Limitations* for a variety of businesses:

1. For a vendor of antique time-pieces, it could be the number of long-case clocks available for sale because they are getting rarer.
2. For a restaurateur: the number of people dining (known as 'covers'), which will in turn be affected by the number and arrangement of tables.
3. For a retail store: the amount of linear feet of shelving.
4. For an out-of-town superstore: the number of parking spaces, because that's what limits the number of customers who can shop there on a busy day.
5. For a printing firm: the number of hours it is possible to run that big expensive machine between set-up and maintenance operations.
6. For an engineering company: the availability of man/machine hours.

It's important that you define these in ways that can readily be understood by the people doing the selling. Taking the examples above, you could quantify them as follows:

1. 12 clocks per year
2. 60 covers across 20 tables per night
3. 500 metre stock movements per week
4. 800 parking place visits per day (assuming each visit takes 2 hours and you open for 8 hours)
5. 60 per minute for 960 machine minutes per day
6. 400 man/machine hours per week

Success is a question of balance

Ultimately, understanding precisely the nature and capacity of the Critical Resource Limitation on the business will govern the direction and amount of promotional activity. What we want to do with our sales-boosting activities is generate just enough business to exactly use up all of the critical resources that are available in any trading period.

- If we sell any more capacity than we have, the business will overheat and fail to deliver, or at best, incur increased costs. Money will also have been wasted in getting those orders that can't be fulfilled.
- If we sell less capacity than we have, then the business is not making as much money as it could be because resources will be lying idle, yet still have to be paid for.

There is another point to be made here. While you should be concerned about the key constraints within your business, spare a thought for your supply chain. If you're buying in goods and services, remember that resource limitations will apply in an equally powerful and negative way to your suppliers and it is crucial for you to understand what they are. If you ever let a customer down, they won't care whether the problem is 'in-house' or a supplier failure — as far as they are concerned, it's just you!

Balancing the sales effort that generates demand, with the supply of limited key resources, is at the very heart of how to successfully grow the profitability of a business.

This is because understanding where the limitation is tells us where we need to concentrate our efforts on making the most money or getting the maximum value from the resources used.

'One Number' Value Added

Identifying the factor that limits the amount you can sell, tells you what is restricting the amount of profit you can make: when you run out of product, or 'people hours' to deliver the service, you have to stop selling (or risk delivery failure) and then you're going to stop making money.

To counter this limitation, you need to make sure that the entire focus of trading activities in your business is on maximising the profit that can be made from each unit of the limiting resource.

This is a fundamental insight and it informs the entire approach of the business. It helps you focus on what you are really selling (as opposed to what the customer is buying), which customers we should be selling to and how prices should be set.

This results in the 'One Number' we have been talking about. For example:

If Jones Ltd has overheads of £720,000 and labour resources of 15,000 hours per year then they have to make £48.00 on every hour just to break-even (£720,000/15,000). To make a reasonable profit they should target on making £64.00 (£48.00/75% for a business in 'safe' trading condition).

The 'One Number' for Jones Ltd. is:

Value Added Per Hour of £64.00

We'll examine how resources, prices and profitability are linked in greater detail in chapters 4 and 5.

Safe Rate of Growth

This is a big one because growth consumes cash[2] and if cash is already tight for your business, then generating a positive cash flow must be an essential part of growth planning. Cash is so important to a business because running out of it will kill the business, so it would be madness to attempt to grow without fully understanding this limitation.

This does *not* mean that you should set out right now to explore new lines of funding, even if you think you can get more credit: rather the opposite. Cash-flow pressures are usually a symptom of other things that are happening *within* the business and it's wise not to go 'outside' the firm to borrow more money unless you have sorted out what is causing the cash drain in the first place.

If the problem is poor profitability, then some of the techniques described in chapters 3, 4 and 5 will definitely help.

For now, let's concentrate on establishing the safe rate at which a business can grow, because if you're trying to grow a business without much cash to start with, you must be aware that there's a maximum safe rate at which sales can be increased. If even a thriving company exceeds that rate, it will find itself a victim of its own success because the increased stock, assets, overheads and working capital demanded by the growth will create a cash shortfall.

To avoid being sucked into expensive borrowings, the business has to keep within a rate of growth that will be self-financed as a result of the profits being generated, which will cover, or exceed, the increased working capital requirements.

The cash that a growing business will have available for growth is determined by a mix of:

- **the timing difference between the payments you have to make and those received, which is called the** *operating cash cycle*
- **the amount of cash required to finance each £ of sales including working capital and operating expenses**
- **the amount of cash generated by each £ of sales**

Together, this mix of factors, determines the *self-financing growth rate*.[3] This is the maximum rate of growth that can be sustained before the trading activities start to suck out more cash than that trade is generating. It is critically important because it is the rate at which the business can sustain its growth through the revenues it is generating before having to resort to borrowing.

Let's see how to calculate the *self-financing growth rate* for Smith and Jones. I want to do both so that you can see how they compare.

We need their profit and loss account:

	Smith Ltd		Jones Ltd	
Sales	£1,200,000		£3,600,000	
Cost of sales	£900,000		£2,844,000	
Gross profit	£300,000	25%	£756,000	21%
Overheads	£240,000		£720,000	
Net profit	£60,000		£36,000	

Figure 2.4

And their balance sheet:

Balance Sheet for Smith Ltd			Balance Sheet for Jones Ltd	
£ 60,000		Fixed assets	£ 116,000	
£ 20,100		Cash at bank	£ 46,300	
£ 148,000		Debtors	£ 650,000	
£ 100,000		Stock	£ 480,000	
£ 268,100		Total current assets	£ 1,176,300	
	£ 328,100	Total assets		£ 1,292,300
£ 148,000		Creditors	£ 520,000	
£ 60,000		Bank loan	£ 500,000	
£ 208,000		Total current liabilities	£ 1,020,000	
	£ 120,100	Total assets less total liabilities		£ 272,300
£ 100		Share capital	£ 300	
£ 120,000		Profit & loss account	£ 272,000	
£ 120,100		Total shareholders funds	£ 272,300	

Figure 2.5

We need both of these tables because some of the figures we require come from each.

Now this and what follows looks like a horribly complicated set of numbers, but if you take it steady and work it through you will find that the principles are fairly obvious. (There is nothing more difficult here than pressing the division key on a calculator, I promise.)

The first thing we need to do is work out how long cash is tied up for in the *operating cash cycle* as follows:

Smith Ltd		Jones Ltd
	Debtor days	
45 days	(calculated by dividing the debtor by the daily sales (sales turnover/365))	66 days
	Stock turnover	
41 days	(calculated by dividing the stock by the daily cost of sales (cost of sales/365))	62 days
	Operating cash cycle	
86 days	(Total debtor & stock days)	128 days
	Creditor days	
60 days	(calculated by dividing the creditors by the daily cost of sales (cost of sales/365))	67 days
26 days	Cash tied up over operating cash cycle (Total debtor & stock days less creditor days)	61 days

Figure 2.6

Next we need to figure out the average amount of cash tied up over the *operating cash cycle* as follows:

Smith Ltd		Jones Ltd
25%	Gross margin from the profit & loss account	21%
	The cost of sales needed to generate £100 of sales	
£ 75	(calculated from £100 x (1 - the gross margin %))	£ 79
	The average amount invested in cost of sales over the operating cash cycle	
	(this calculated from the amount of cost of sales x the proportion of the operating	
	cash cycle for which the cash required to finance it (cost of sales needed per £100 x	
£ 22	(cash tied up/operating cash cycle))	£ 38
20%	Overheads as a proportion of sales are overheads/sales	20%
£ 20	So for every £100 of sales the overhead invested is 100 x % overhead	£ 20
	Assume the cash needed for overheads over the cycle	
£ 10	on average is /2	£ 10
	The average amount of cash tied up per £100 of sales in total over the operating	
	cash cycle is = cash required to finance stock + cash	
£ 32	needed to finance overheads	£ 48

Figure 2.7

So far so good ... Now we can get to that important number, the *self-financing growth rate*:

Smith Ltd		Jones Ltd
5%	The net profit margin (net profit/sales)	1%
£ 32	Divided by the amount of cash tied up per £100 of sales	£ 48
15.6%	**Self-financing growth rate**	2.1%
	Operating cycles per year	
4.3	(365/operating cash cycle days)	2.9
	Annual self-financing growth rate	
65.8%	(Operating cycles per year x self-financing growth rate)	6.0%

Figure 2.8

What this means is, that at the current levels of profitability, Smith Ltd can plan to grow their business by 65% to £1,980,00 next year and Jones Ltd by 6% to £3,816,000. If either of them grows any more than that without increasing profitability or reducing the *operating cash cycle*, they will have a very high risk of running out of cash.

This knowledge is crucially important for Jones Ltd because they are unlikely to be able to borrow any more money, as there is insufficient security on the balance sheet for the comfort of a lender.

(By the way, notice how the *self-financing growth rate* is calculated from the net profit and you quickly realise why I suggest growing profit before sales in most cases. Growing sales on thin margins consumes cash very quickly.)

Now I want you to take a deep breath and, using the examples above, work out the *self-financing growth rate* for your own business. (All right, get your accountant to do it if you must.)

When you have done that, make a commitment not to exceed it without first figuring out where you can get the extra cash you will need to do so!

Notes/ References

1. Warnes B (1984) *The Ghenghis Khan guide to business* Osmosis Publications, London p.19
2. Churchill N C & Mullins J (2001) *How fast can your company afford to grow?* Harvard Business Review May.
3. Churchill N C & Mullins J W (2001) *How fast can your company afford to grow?* Harvard Business Review May p.136.

3 THE EASIEST WAYS TO GROW A BUSINESS

Customers should be at the centre of all business activity. Here, we'll look at how we are going to grow the business through our existing customers before we try to find some new ones. All the background thinking we've done this far has been crucial, though, as it's so important to understand that boosting sales is something that should be done only *after* you have worked out for your business the:

- break-even point
- Critical Resource Limitation
- 'One Number' for your business
- safe rate of growth

Remember that it is profits we are trying to grow before anything else because maximising the profitability of the current level of trade is what will be used to fund further growth, without external borrowings, if done correctly.

Those precautionary points in the last chapter give us a number of clues about the ways in which we might grow that are alternatives to the methods you may already heard of.

There are the established ways to grow and there are the shoestring ways to grow . . .

Established ways to grow

Established marketing principles suggest that there are four ways to grow a business, although not all of them will be appropriate if cash is tight:

1. **acquisition: buy another business in the same market**
2. **increase the average value of each sales order by persuading each customer to spend more every time they do business with you by offering them:**

   - **alternative established products and services**
   - **new products and services developed to suit their needs**

3. **increase the frequency of purchase from each customer by finding ways to persuade customers to do business with you more often**
4. **increase the number of customers; effective marketing should generate new business according to the conversion rate of prospective customer (prospects) into actual customers, which can be done by offering them:**

   - **established products and services**
   - **new products and services developed to suit the market needs**

Acquisition

This is a well-established mechanism for achieving growth quickly. The potential benefits include gaining access to more customers and being able to tap into increased resources quickly.

The trouble is that this route is rarely cheap and never easy. The problems of integrating different firms often go unrecognised in the euphoria and anticipation of the event, and most people only discover how hard it actually is to make two disparate cultures work as one when they try and do it.

Acquisition is high cost and high risk, so it's obviously out of the question if we haven't got the money or can't afford to lose what we have. It would not not sensible to try and borrow money on the off-chance we could make an acquisition work, especially if our own business model is still not producing enough profit to fund ideas like that.

Acquisition should only be attempted when your business is cash-rich, stable and seeking the sort of leverage that can come from quickly gaining more of the market or offering complimentary products and services. This is not a shoestring strategy.

Stick to what you're good at

If money is tight, and you are an established business, committed to growing on a shoestring, then the lowest-risk, lowest-cost approach is to deal in what you know about, as illustrated in the figure opposite.

Finding new customers is always hard, as is selling them something you've not tried before, so this option is going to be expensive and risky. It is another reason why so many start-ups fail: 8% die within the first year and 29% have failed within 3 years (see Introduction). This is because the entire business model is geared towards finding new customers for new products and services.

Developing new products and services might seem attractive, particularly if you are feeling the pinch in your marketplace and feel that you can steal a march on the competition. It is often the route taken by businesses that pride themselves on innovation.

		A Established Customers	B New Customers	
New Ones	1	New products or services	New products or services	Hard
Established Products & Services	2	Increase frequency of purchase	Established products and services	Easier
	3	Additional established product or service		
	4	Superior product or service of same type		
	5	Accessory product or service		
	6	More of the same product or service per transaction		
		Easier	Harder	

Figure 3.1

It can be even more tempting if you have recognised a need in an existing customer. However, be warned that this is not a strategy to follow if you already have too few customers making up a large proportion of your turnover. The last thing you want to do in this situation is increase the concentration of risk further. Unfortunately, some firms get sucked into trying this because it is so hard to get a relationship going with a potential customer that it is tempting to try and sell them anything.

The time to get involved with developing new products and services is when you have a nice large and loyal customer base and are trying to figure out what else to sell them next. They can also help to pay for any development costs.

There are several reasons that make selling new products and services harder to either established customers or new customers. These include:

- credibility gaps
- confidence gaps
- training gaps
- support gaps

- risk of failure
- development cost
- higher cost to supply
- unknown factors

I'm sure you can think of others from your own industry perspective.

So our best chances of growing a shoestring business using established methods are in the bottom of columns A and B in Figure 3.1:

- **A2–A6 maximising the level of business and profitability with existing customers through established products and services**
- **B2 finding new customers for your established products and services**

Maximise existing customer value: The triple effect

The triple effect is what happens when small increases in sales are achieved in each of three ways simultaneously:

1. **Increasing the amount sold at each customer transition.**
2. **Increase purchase frequency by persuading customers to do business with you more often.**
3. **Increasing the number of customers.**

If we can get just 5% additional sales from each of these methods then aiming for 20% growth no longer seems such a great leap, does it?

Increasing the number of customers is very important because, as well as the boost to sales and profitability, it reduces the concentration risk. In other words, your business is less dependent upon a small number of buyers. However, achieving this is never simple, easy or cost free: so we will work on that later.

For now, let's concentrate on increasing the amount of each sale and frequency of sale to existing customers. These two techniques are all about improving the productivity of your transactions with each customer. Then we will examine how to improve *profitability* by selectively working with them.

If we can simultaneously improve gross margin . . . your profits will go through the roof!

By concentrating on existing customers first, growing a business may be easier than you think! The trick is to understand that small changes are important.

Nurture existing customers

Increasing the number of customers is what everyone in business is trying to do to maintain and grow market share. No customer lasts for ever and therefore those that are disappearing need replacing.

Maximising growth and profitability with existing is by far the easiest of all our options for two reasons:

1. we need to make sure that we nurture our existing profitable customers as best we can before we go courting new ones. The trouble is that prospecting for new work is distracting and. and it is easy to forget to attend to your loyal customers. Before you know it, they will be wooed away somewhere else.

2. new customers can be difficult to find, as you are probably well aware. We definitely need them, but it costs five to fifteen times more to get business from a

new customer than it does from an existing one.[1] The reason for this is that it requires marketing effort, which costs time and money.[2]

So when thinking about ways to boost sales on a shoestring, the first place to look is at our existing customers, which will be more profitable because our selling costs are going to be lower.[3]

I'll come back to ways of finding new customers later, because it's a big subject and needs a whole section on its own. For now, let's look at ways to grow that are less expensive.

Increasing the amount of each sale

You could try to **increase the amount of products** purchased each time just a little bit – say 10% – by persuading each customer to spend more every time they do business with you. This is sometimes called 'up-selling'. It's cost a lot to get a customer to the point where they will buy, but once they're there, it won't cost anything extra to try to get them to buy something else. There are four ways to do it (using the columns A and B from figure 3.1) and I call it the 'size, fries amd pies' mode:

- A6 sell more of the same product or service per transaction. In a burger bar, for example, you might be asked if you would like to 'super-size' that order.
- A5 sell some accessories ('. . . and would you like fries with that?').
- A4 sell a superior, more expensive version of the same thing ('. . . the quarter pounder with cheese is only a little more').
- A3 use the existing relationship to sell additional products ('. . . and how about an apple pie for dessert?').

Increasing sales frequency

- A2 Next, see if you can find ways to persuade customers to do business with you more often, say from 20 to 21 times a year, or a 5% increase. This is also very important because increasing the frequency of purchase, if done correctly, improves the likelihood of you keeping the customer. So the same customer spends more and stays with you for longer. There are a number of ways to do this:

    - think about what kind of offer you could make to encourage a next visit. Examples include free dessert with next meal or discount with next purchase. One reason this works well is that the voucher they keep to redeem the offer is a constant reminder.

    - make contact more often. If you increase the frequency of communications and remind customers of what they need, they'll buy from you more frequently. If you have a large customer base, concentrate on the 20% who contribute most profits, using methods such as e-mails (make sure you have permission first), letters, phone calls or meetings.

    - work on your 'back end'. For example, people who buy machines need maintenance, supplies, spare parts and all sorts of other things. A firm of general mechanical engineers started to make water filters, a difficult business because each customer buys only one per household. They then hit on the idea of selling the chemicals directly and now their customers buy from them every six months. Suddenly they are making more on the chemicals than the machines – so what business are they in?

- make it more convenient to buy from you. I'm sure you've experienced numerous occasions when you knew what you wanted to buy and where you wanted to buy it from, but it just seemed too difficult for the vendor to take your money. In the retail world, this includes things like the shop assistant who was too busy to serve you, the barman whose eye you couldn't catch and the website that wouldn't accept a payment. In business-to-business situations, it can be made worse with complex contractual arrangements: make sure you're not asking your customers to jump through un-necessary hoops to deal with you. Remember that real people like things real easy!
- work on the relationship. If your customers are buying from several sources at once, improving the quality of the relationship that you have with them will help you gain an edge over the competition.

Now if we can simultaneously improve gross margin to produce a quadruple effect . . . your profits will go through the roof!

The way to grow on a shoestring

We've looked at the established ways to grow a business; now let's concentrate on the shoestring ways to grow.

The shoestring way is to focus on growing profitably and generating cash rather than increasing market share in terms of turnover or the number of customers.

Its success depends on two factors: the first is the profitability of the customer; the second is the profitability of the various roducts and services our business provides, which we'll come to later.

Not all customers are equal

We have established that developing existing customers to maximise their value as a source of revenue and profits is likely to be one of the best ways to boost sales when money is tight.

Well, yes, but there is a potential problem with pursuing this strategy. Not all customers are equal, and it is quite common to discover that the customers who are creating the most sales turnover are not the same ones who are producing the most profits.

The quality of the relationship between you, the supplier, and the customer can vary enormously. This has profound effects on:

- the amount of trade
- the profitability of this trade and therefore the value of the customer to the business
- the amount of precious resources consumed in supplying each different customer

In a nutshell, some customers are very much better for a business than others. Those who are 'difficult', or who tend to switch suppliers frequently, are going to be more expensive to develop (and therefore have a different value to the business) than those who are loyal and easy to deal with. Before deciding who you want to keep you need to understand existing customers in terms of their turnover, profitability and the resources they consume so that you can decide which ones to grow your business with.

Digging for customer platinum

Every business should have key customers – the stalwarts who provide us with most of our steady stream of income.

Key customers can usually be defined as the 20% who provide us with 80% of our business. However, this calculation is often based on the amount of turnover generated from each customer and you'll often find that, because of the customer's strength in this relationship (buyer power) or longevity of the relationship (during which time prices are likely to have been pushed down), the profitability picture is very different. Normally, the customers who are giving your business the lion's share of sales turnover are not the same ones who are giving you the lion's share of the profits.

So you need to be looking at each customer from the point of view of the amount of gross profit that each one generates (your accountant should be able to get this information quickly for you if you don't already know). Now apply the 80:20 rule again. Is it the same group of customers? I'll bet it isn't! These are the ones who are truly your key accounts: the customers who are providing the most profitable income are the ones you should be spending the most time and effort nurturing.

- **80% of your *sales* are probably coming from 20% of your customers**
- **80% of your *profits* are probably coming from 20% of your customers**
- **You'll often find that customers in each group are different**

With our existing set of customers what we want to do is:

1. **Identify which are the most profitable and work to increase the business we do with them as previously described. The single most important way of achieving this is to increase the frequency and quality of**

communication with these key accounts. You should be in touch with your top earners at least two to three times per month.

2. With the less profitable customers we want to increase profitability before committing our precious resources to doing more work for them at low margins. This is about getting the price right and we'll be addressing that shortly.

3. With customers below a certain level of profitability, where we cannot increase the margin for some reason, what we need to do is . . . get rid of them! It sounds awful, but let someone else have the problem because it is only by releasing our key resources to work on more profitable business that we can grow profitably.

To sort this out, we need to examine each customer based on the amount of gross profit they are generating and the resources consumed, and then tabulate them accordingly.

An easy way to do this is with a simple spreadsheet table. You can then sort by customer sales per annum (descending) or gross profit (descending). The resources column can be a guess (accountants can hardly ever provide this information unprepared) so long as it is expressed as something meaningful for your business.

Below is the sort of picture you might see for Jones Ltd, sorted first by descending sales, then by descending gross profit. Don't be put off because there are a lot of numbers – think of it like soil; there may be a lot of grit but we are looking for any silver, gold or platinum, which should be easy to spot if you know how.

Customers sorted by sales and profit

Customers sorted by sales (descending)

Customer ID	Sales per Annum	Gross Profit per Annum	Gross Margin %	% Resources Used
x	£ 392,000	£ 27,440	7.0%	25%
l	£ 300,000	£ 48,000	16.0%	20%
p	£ 240,000	£ 84,000	35.0%	4%
t	£ 224,000	£ 31,360	14.0%	5%
h	£ 200,000	£ 18,000	9.0%	4%
ae	£ 180,000	£ 27,000	15.0%	3%
af	£ 134,000	£ 46,900	35.0%	2%
ab	£ 110,000	£ 33,000	30.0%	3%
g	£ 104,000	£ 13,520	13.0%	2%
a	£ 100,000	£ 23,000	23.0%	2%
m	£ 98,000	£ 26,460	27.0%	1.5%
q	£ 94,000	£ 30,080	32.0%	2%
w	£ 92,000	£ 27,600	30.0%	1%
v	£ 76,000	£ 19,760	26.0%	1%
k	£ 72,000	£ 20,880	29.0%	1%
s	£ 72,000	£ 9,360	13.0%	1%
y	£ 56,000	£ 15,120	27.0%	1%
n	£ 46,000	£ 13,340	29.0%	1%
ag	£ 40,000	£ 15,600	39.0%	2%
b	£ 20,000	£ 4,600	23.0%	2%
u	£ 16,000	£ 640	4.0%	0.01%
z	£ 12,000	£ 3,360	28.0%	1.5%
e	£ 5,200	£ 2,912	56.0%	1%
Other examples to total…				
£ 3,600,000	£ 756,000	21.0%	100%	

Customers sorted by gross profit (descending)

Customer ID	Sales per Annum	Gross Profit per Annum	Gross Margin %	% Resources Used
p	£ 240,000	£ 84,000	35.0%	4%
l	£ 300,000	£ 48,000	16.0%	20%
af	£ 134,000	£ 46,900	35.0%	2%
ab	£ 110,000	£ 33,000	30.0%	3%
t	£ 224,000	£ 31,360	14.0%	5%
q	£ 94,000	£ 30,080	32.0%	2%
w	£ 92,000	£ 27,600	30.0%	1%
x	£ 392,000	£ 27,440	7.0%	25%
ae	£ 180,000	£ 27,000	15.0%	3%
m	£ 98,000	£ 26,460	27.0%	1.5%
a	£ 100,000	£ 23,000	23.0%	2%
k	£ 72,000	£ 20,880	29.0%	1%
v	£ 76,000	£ 19,760	26.0%	1%
h	£ 200,000	£ 18,000	9.0%	4%
ag	£ 40,000	£ 15,600	39.0%	2%
y	£ 56,000	£ 15,120	27.0%	1%
g	£ 104,000	£ 13,520	13.0%	2%
n	£ 46,000	£ 13,340	29.0%	1%
s	£ 72,000	£ 9,360	13.0%	1%
b	£ 20,000	£ 4,600	23.0%	2%
z	£ 12,000	£ 3,360	28.0%	1.5%
e	£ 5,200	£ 2,912	56.0%	1%
u	£ 16,000	£ 640	4.0%	0.01%
Other examples to total…				
£ 3,600,000	£ 756,000	21.0%	100%	

Figure 3.2

From this example, you'll quickly observe that customer 'x' is ranked 1st on sales but much lower on gross profit contribution. They are providing only 3.6% of the profits (£27,440), yet are taking up a quarter of the organisation's resources. Customer 'p' however, is ranked 3rd on turnover but 1st on profit contribution. Even more importantly, this customer is only consuming 4% of the resources but generating 11% of the gross profit (£84,000 / £756,000). Now that's what I call a key account!

Let's imagine these are the results from our example company, Jones Ltd. Whatever action they decide to take, they must *not* attempt to boost sales from customer 'x', or from customer 'l' (second on the list) for that matter. The combination of low gross margins and high-resources consumption would make this suicidal! Doubling the business from customers 'x' and 'l' will consume 90% of their resources, thus preventing them fulfilling the orders from more profitable customers, yet only earning £75,440 of extra gross profit. Because the extra work leaves only 10% of their capacity for supplying their more profitable customers, Jones Ltd are suddenly going to find out that they will be unable to cover the overheads.

This is a very important point because it happens all the time. Seemingly important, high-volume customers can prevent you serving the more profitable ones effectively.

Thought for the day: what would happen to profitability if Jones Ltd lost customer 'x'? The answer is not much. Even though 'x' *seems* very important because his £392k is 11% of the turnover for this group and he is consuming a lot of effort (which makes him look large on the operations radar), the profit generated is only about £27k or less than 4% of the £756k total contribution. This is an amount Jones Ltd could stand to lose without too much of a problem – it would be of even less concern if their break-even point was right.

Here is a bigger thought for the day: what if Jones Ltd lost customer 'x' and replaced them with six customers of type 'p' consuming about the same amount of resource? Hmm ... so £27k goes out of the window but 6 × £84k (which is £504,000) replaces it – increasing the total contribution from £756k to over £1.2 million. That's the way to do it!

I'm not suggesting you can attain that sort of improvement overnight – you can't. But it does powerfully illustrate the sales direction for the business. It also shows that looking at profitability from the key constraining resources' point of view provides a crucial clue to the sort of customers we should be looking after and looking for.

It's common to discover that many of the customers that generate the least profit are those we find difficult to deal with and who soak up most time and resources – the nightmare customers we put up with because they are so 'important' to the business. These are not key accounts. What we need to be doing with them is either tactically managing the relationship until they become less of a burden, or nudging up the prices until they start making you some money or decide to go elsewhere. If they become a key account, the bother is worth it; if not, letting them go will free up resources that you can then deploy on more profitable clients.

This is an important insight that challenges much of the given wisdom on the importance of customer retention, but it's true nonetheless. You won't be able to boost sales on a budget if all your resources are tied up servicing customers who don't pay you much more than it costs you to supply them.

The one-customer company

What if your business is one of those where most of your sales go to *one* customer? Obviously you cannot be selective in treatment in the way just described. Having just one individual or organisation which generates most of the profit for your business is a high-risk situation: the stories of relatively successful businesses that have suddenly gone under because of the pressure tactics of their one important customer are legion. As a general rule of thumb, no more than 20% of your gross profit should be coming from one customer. Provided that no customer is contributing more than 20% of your profit AND that your trading gross margin is set up correctly at as much above 20% as your market sector will stand, then it should be possible to survive the loss of any one major customer for as long as it takes to replace them.

If you are actually in the position where you have one customer who is delivering more than 20% of your gross profit:

- check that you are doing everything possible to keep their business for the time being
- get some new customers *fast*

If the trading characteristics of your market are such that gross margins are much lower than 20%, please do two things:

1. keep overheads as low as is consistent with a healthy break-even point as described earlier. You'll be very vulnerable otherwise.
2. don't nurture major account customers only. Make sure that you have lots of customers and keep topping up your customer base so that if any of them drift away, you're not fatally holed.

Notes/ References

1. Frazer-Robinson, J. (1999). *Building Customer Loyalty*, David Grant Publishing.
2. Barsky, (1994). *World Class Customer Satisfaction*, Irwin Professional. Peppers, D, & Rogers, M. (1993). *The One to One Future: Building Relationships One Customer at a Time*, Doubleday. Reichheld, F. & Sasser, W. E. Jr (1990). 'Zero defections: Quality comes to services', *Harvard Business Review*, Sep-Oct.
3. Birch, E. N. (1990). *Focus on value in creating customer satisfaction*, The Conference Board, 304 Research Report No. 944, New York.

4 GETTING THE PRICE RIGHT

We know that some customers are highly motivated by value for money and, as a result, are the most fickle. They might *say* that quality and service are more important – but don't believe it!

Price is always important to fickle customers. Even if you concentrate on meeting their needs, they will always be trying to get a better deal than they got from you last time. Eventually, if you persist in trying to sell to them, they will grind your profit margin down with threats and comparisons with the competition until you just can't go any lower. Then they will move on to someone who's cheaper, and there will always be someone else who will give away a little more margin for a little more business.

If you persist in dealing with customers like this, you'll end up attracting more of them because your whole style of business will become focused on offering the lowest prices, which means meagre profits on each sale. When things are as tight as that, the only thing keeping you afloat will be the huge volume of trade you need to do to cover your overheads with those ridiculously low margins. Lose one big customer and you are dead.

But getting the lowest price isn't important to everyone:[1]

■ **10–14% of the population buy the cheapest goods on offer**

- **80% buy value**
- **5% buy expensive because they can afford 'the best' and, to them, a high price represents high value**

Unless you operate in a 'perfect' market, where the laws of supply and demand affect the price of a commodity, there is always room to appeal to customers who value what you're selling – and value it enough to pay a little more for it because you are different from the competition.

If you don't believe me, go out into the street and watch some cars going past. You'll see both the cheapest models on offer – such as ancient Ladas from the former Eastern Bloc – as well as small and basic ones from the Far East. But what is the proportion of drivers who have chosen to spend as little as possible compared with those who are driving much more expensive marques such as Mercedes, BMW, Range Rover?

How many of those drivers were wearing watches made by TAG, Rolex or Omega compared with those wearing Seiko or Swatch? These people may be concerned with getting good value, but they are not interested in the lowest cost car or watch or probably anything else for that matter.

Exciting isn't it? That simple test tells you that where there is difference: there is money to be made and it is our job to make as much of it as possible.

The great thing about business is that there is no such thing as a 'perfect market'. The whole point about markets is that they are made up of buyers and sellers all looking for an 'edge' and, at any one time, someone has more of an edge than the others. In these circumstances, deals take place.

There is one golden rule to establishing the right price for anything and that is that the customer will only ever pay what they think it is worth for them.

> I once went to a market on the island of Bali, Indonesia where the stallholders were proffering all manner of eastern delights. Many were offering similar articles and one could move freely amongst the stallholders and haggle to get the best deal. The 'perfect market', you may very well think.
>
> I left the market clutching my prizes in the plastic bags provided with each purchase. 'Wow,' said our guide to me, 'You did well.' What do you mean? 'Well, you got three black-and-white striped bags, one black one and a green one!' So? 'Well if you beat the stallholder down to his bottom price he puts your purchase into a black-and-white striped bag, if you got close you get a black one, the green is average.' So you mean to tell me, that from the first transaction, I am clutching a bag that announces I am a mean negotiator? 'Yup, did you notice there were stalls where you didn't get such good attention? Americans on the tour get a lot of red bags; market people like them better than you.'

I was totally lost in admiration for the system's guile, simplicity and effectiveness. Someone will always find a way to get an edge and when you run your own business, it's your job to be that someone.

However, in more sophisticated markets you can struggle to win. For example, I once went from stall to stall in a market in Singapore bargaining on a lace tablecloth that was highly prized by my wife. They all seemed the same but I quickly reached a price below which no-one was prepared to sell – so I bought it. Smiling, the vendor took me to the back of the shop and offered tea, where he also showed me the video system that had faithfully recorded my wife's original interest and my futile excursions attempting to negotiate a price around all the all the stalls he ran in the marketplace (about 80% of them).

Clever . . . huh? You can't win them all I suppose. That's quite an important point, actually; if you are not winning where you are, then move on to somewhere where you can.

Those examples describe buying experiences. Now let's look at things from a seller's perspective.

Flexing prices

Small businesses are so often cautious about flexing prices, for apparently good reasons:

- we are intimidated by the big extremes between pleasure and pain
- we fear that we might lose more customers than we can afford
- we don't really understand what motivates our customers
- we under-value our skills
- we tend to calculate price according to what things *cost*, rather than what they are worth
- many of us don't really understand the numbers or how to work them in our favour

So let's explore what happens to sales, profits and production when prices are varied . . .

The discounting catastrophe

One of the things that every business experiences from time to time is price pressure. Try not to give in – it can be catastrophic, for the reasons outlined here.

Let's say a customer asks you to give another 5% discount in exchange for an order before the end of the month. (This is an old trick, but a good one: sales people are often under pressure to meet their targets by key accounting dates). The problem is, that giving away that 5% will cause your gross margin to drop massively out of proportion if your margins are thin in the first place.

This is how it happens in practice:

> Your business sells for £120 something that costs £90 to produce, generating a gross profit of £30. The gross margin is 25% (£30/£120).
>
> If you discount the selling price by 5% so that it drops to £114, the cost to you will not change but the gross profit drops from £30 to £24 and the gross margin tumbles to 21% (£24/£114).

The *relative* decrease in gross margin is disproportionately high at 16%: (25%–21%)/25%.

The price discount/volume trap

This is only part of the story, though. The really dangerous effect of discounting is the impact on volume which must go up if the business tries to make the same profit as before but on discounted prices.

Consider the scenario in Figure 4.1, in which a business, feeling it needs to react to market pressure, reduces prices across the board by

5%. You can see that the effect of the price reduction, if the unit volume of sales remains the same, is to completely wipe out the net profit.

To restore net profit to the previous level, turnover will need to be increased by 19%. Because the units are now sold for 95% of what they were before, though, this means that the business would have to increase its production by a massive 25% in volume terms to get the same profitability from a 5% reduction in price. To put some flesh on these bones:

- Let's say that before the price cut, each unit sold for £12. The business needed to make and sell 100 to achieve a sales turnover of £1,200.
- Cutting the prices by 5% means that turnover has to increase to £1,428 to get back to a net profit of £60. Follow this through and you will understand why:

  - each unit now sells for £11.40 (£12 less 5% discount)
  - the cost of sales remains the same at £9 so we only make £2.40 on each sale instead of the £3 we were making before
  - to make the £3 we were originally making we have to sell 1.25 units to get back to our starting position (£3/ £2.40)
  - so the business needs to make and sell 125 units instead of 100
  - 125 units sold at £11.40 brings us to the £1,428 turnover figure

The profit account for each position looks like this:

	Original Prices		5% Reduction		Sales Needed	
Sales	1200		1140		1428	25% more units required just to stand still!
Cost of sales	900		900		1128	
Gross profit	300	25%	240	21%	300	
Overheads	240		240		240	
Net profit	60		0		60	

Figure 4.1

The 'pile 'em high and sell 'em cheap' tactic may be good if you have a high volume of stock to shift to make room in your warehouse. On the other hand, if the supply of products comes from a factory with production constraints or a service organisation that is limited to the number of hours that people can work, you can imagine that the demand could quickly outstrip the production capability of the organisation.

So what happens to profits next if the cost of sales is increased by the need to pay overtime or shift-working premiums? To paraphrase Stuart Rose, chief executive of Marks and Spencer, it makes us 'busy fools'!

This is why your response to any request for a discount should always be to challenge it.

■ **Lower expectations. You rarely see a Rolex watch in a shop window with a price ticket that says 'or nearest offer', do you? So don't invite a request for discount by giving the impression that you will be open to offers. Respond to such a request by giving the impression that you hardly ever need to discount because your product/ service is so popular. Let the customer know that this is such an unusual request that you will have to consider it carefully, check your figures, whatever. Anything to create the impression that you are not going to give in lightly and even then only a little.**

■ Play for time and information. Say 'I can see why you might ask that. Just so that I can help you best, can I ask you a couple of questions?' Well handled, this might reveal more about the benefits to the customer and allow you to defend the attack on your price with good grace.

■ Ask why they want it. The answer may seem obvious, but while you're discussing price there are three crucial variables in any negotiation: power, time and information.[2] Asking why someone wants a price reduction does several things:

■ it obliges them to justify their position and puts them 'on the back foot' while they think about it

■ informs you about the strength of their negotiating position

■ creates the impression that you do not give away discounts without a reason

■ gives you time to think of a response (preferably something other than giving in to the request)

■ Don't concede; trade instead. Ask for something in return, rather than give something away for nothing. Giving away discounts always devalues your product in the mind of the customer and sends a signal that you were probably charging too much in the first place. It is much better to emphasise your value and fair pricing by bargaining down what you are offering in response. In other words don't change the price, change the package.[3] This can work well if you take off something that is of little value to your customer but saves you a lot of money. Try something like:

- 'Well, if you *really* can't afford it, I could reduce price by x% *if* we modified our usual three-year guarantee to only one year. After all, the product is very reliable . . .'
- 'If we staggered the deliveries, it would mean that we could cut over-time and I could offer you a saving then . . .'
- 'We might be able to do something if you were to agree to early payment terms . . .' (This is my favourite because it helps with cash flow.)

You get the picture.

Formal negotiations such as tender submissions and the like are just the same. You defend your price with a value proposition focused on the customer's wants and needs.

Increasing price and profitability

Even a relatively small price increase can have an important side-effect, which is a dramatic improvement in the gross profit return. It is the opposite of the discounting scenario and the arguments are the same but inverted.

To illustrate, let's say that our business sells for £120 something that cost £90 to produce, generating a gross profit of £30. The gross margin is 25% (£30/£120), as in the previous example.

Now if you increase prices by 5%, the selling price becomes £126 (£120 × 1.05). The cost remains the same, so the gross profit is now £36 and the gross margin is 28.5% (£36/ £126.00).

BUT the *relative* increase in gross margin is higher at 14%: (28.5%−25%)/25%). This is very good for the business.

What I really like about this effect is that the actual amount of cash left in the till after the sale is disproportionately much higher as well. Before prices went up, the business was making £30 on the sale. After the increase, it made £36 because costs remained the same. That's an extra £6 or a cash increase of 20% for a 5% increase in prices: (£36−£30)/£30. A significant positive cash benefit.

This happens because any improvement in gross margin % is multiplied by the turnover. The reason I point that out is because it is a very important thing to understand for businesses that have a high turnover but low gross margins. Say our two example companies, Smith and Jones, each increase their prices by 5%. Jones is three times better off because the turnover is three times higher:

	Smith Ltd		Jones Ltd	
Sales	£ 1,260,000		£ 3,780,000	
Cost of sales	£ 900,000		£ 2,844,000	
Gross profit	£ 360,000	29%	£ 936,000	25%
Overheads	£ 240,000		£ 720,000	
Net profit	£ 120,000		£ 216,000	
Sales	£ 1,200,000		£ 3,600,000	
Cost of sales	£ 900,000		£ 2,844,000	
Gross profit	£ 300,000	25%	£ 756,000	21%
Overheads	£ 240,000		£ 720,000	
Net profit	£ 60,000		£ 36,000	
Profit improvement	£ 60,000		£ 180,000	

Figure 4.2

The effect is most valuable where the gross margin % is low in the first place. This extreme sensitivity of profits to turnover volume and gross margin % is the reason why the gross margin % figure is such a key indicator for financial analysts.

Try working out what a 5% increase in prices would do for the profitability of your business. You can do this easily by first laying out the figures from your own profit and loss account as indicated for Smith Ltd above before the increase, then add 5% to the sales figure but leave cost of sales and overheads as they are. Re-do the sums as indicated in Smith Ltd after the increase, then compare the difference in net profit.

The price increase/volume benefit

Once again, this is only part of the story. The really beneficial effect of increasing prices, even slightly, is the impact on volume if the business is to try and stand still by making the same profit as before on the original prices.

Now consider the scenario in Figure 4.3, in which our business decides to increase prices by 5%. Observe that if sales remain the same the net profit is doubled!

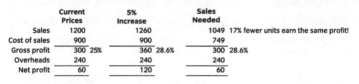

	Current Prices		5% Increase		Sales Needed	
Sales	1200		1260		1049	17% fewer units earn the same profit!
Cost of sales	900		900		749	
Gross profit	300	25%	360	28.6%	300	28.6%
Overheads	240		240		240	
Net profit	60		120		60	

Figure 4.3

But you might argue that increasing prices will probably lose us some customers and you might be right. So how many customers can we afford to lose before this decision hits the previous bottom-line figure?

Well, the sales turnover needed would be reduced by 13% to £1,409. BUT since each product is selling for 5% more, the actual number of units it is necessary to sell is only 75% of what it was before.

This is because say each unit sold for £12 at current prices and then we needed to make and sell 100 to achieve a sales turnover of £1,200. The effect of the 5% price increase meant that turnover could decrease to £1,049 to get back to a net profit of £60. But now each unit sells for £12.60 (£12 plus 5% increase). So to achieve the £1,049 turnover we need only to make and sell 83 units (£1,049/£12.60).

The production requirement is reduced by 17%, so if this were a manufacturing business the company could pretty much take Friday as a holiday!

Or, to answer the original question, if you increased prices by 5% and lost as many as 10% of your customers as a consequence, you would still make more money. In the above example, the net profit would increase to £68.80 for 10% less sales. Go ahead and work it out for yourself.

Although customers can be fickle, the real-life outcome is likely to be very much better than you'd feared. This is because, in deregulated industries, which are those operating in a free market, on average a 5% price increase results in only 2% of customers leaving.[4]

Price, demand, profit and production are locked together

What the above illustrates is that 'flexing' prices across the board by offering discounts or applying increases to the gross margin percentage on a global basis has disproportionately powerful effects on profitability and production 'strain'.

The trouble is that small businesses can only have a limited effect on the market. There is a danger with some businesses that their products or services can become 'commoditised': this means there is little distinction between you and anyone else that produces the same thing. For example, iron, oil and coal are commodities, so their value is decided on the open market according to the laws of supply and demand. If there's a shortage, the price goes up; if we get more out of the ground, the price reduces. There's little that can be done to influence the price because there's is nothing distinguishing or special about a commodity that people would be prepared to pay more for.

If your product becomes commoditised and you have to respond to market forces with global price changes, then beware: there's no guaranteed way of predicting the actual effect of an 'across the board' price variation. The thing you *can* be certain of in a free market is that there'll always be a tendency to pinch profitability and pressurise production into delivering the most for the money paid for it.

But there is some good news. Small businesses, particularly those involved in manufacturing or providing services, are only partly influenced by the 'global' market forces and rarely commoditised to the extent described below. Provided there is a focus on servicing a particular market segment, there will often be opportunities to selectively vary prices to suit the local supply and demand.

I once took a taxi from my hotel at the airport to Kuwait City for which I was charged 40 Kuwait dinars.

While I was enjoying the sights it began to rain, which is unusual there. I found a taxi to take me back to the hotel and it was the same driver. Nonetheless, in the usual way I confirmed the price for the journey before I got in – 'Not 40 dinars,' he said. 'The price to return is 60 dinars.' 'Why is the price different, the distance has not changed?' I enquired. 'Taxi is more expensive in the rain because there are not many taxis and you are getting wet.' Simple; I paid.

Notice that this has nothing to do with the cost of production, the running costs of the cab had not changed one iota – his pricing policy was that the price should rise and fall according to how badly you wanted to ride in his taxi. It was the law of supply and demand in action and perfectly illustrates how price is affected by all the other factors that influence the value for the customer:

- **where something has to be available**
- **when it is required**
- **the circumstances of its availability**

The taxi story also illuminates two other points. Firstly, while the taxi industry may be pretty much the same the world over, that segment which was in Kuwait (defined by its geography and local operating conditions) operated very differently to the one in London where we get rained on all the time and prices are regulated by the meter. Secondly, the place to make money is in the segment you have focused on and when people are prepared to pay it.

So a **dynamic** approach to pricing is required. Dynamic pricing differs from across the board 'price flexing' because the price varies according to the momentary value of the opportunity for the buyer and seller. A dynamic pricing approach recognises that prices may need to change frequently and reactively to respond to all the factors in the market that affect the customers' inclination to buy *at the time a sale is possible*.

The heart of the matter

There is a hidden and powerful reason for taking a dynamic approach to pricing, which was not immediately clear from the taxi story but is nonetheless very important. It is that the taxi driver has only very limited resources, which are himself and his taxi. To maximise profits, he needs to get the most value possible from that resource in every instant of every day. In practice, this meant that he increased his price when it rained or he was the only taxi available and reduced his prices to pick up what trade he could when there was competition or little demand (because an empty taxi is not earning money).

The lesson is that price is important to everyone and the relationship between price, demand, production capacity and profit is immutable.

In any production or service business, the insight that profitability and production are linked is very powerful because:

The way to maximise profits is to adjust prices so that the demand exactly balances the production or resource capacity.

Any less demand, and unused production capacity will incur costs that are not covered by earnings. Any more demand, and production will not keep up or the costs will rise to increase capacity so that the demand can be satisfied – assuming that is possible.

It is this balance that it is at the very heart of boosting profitable sales if you're on a tight budget, so you need to ensure the available production capacity is fully consumed by the customers who are prepared to pay the most for it.

Balancing resources and demand guides our sales activity, which we'll come to later. We must gear promotional and sales activities to keeping the production capacity fully occupied while maximising the gross profit from the sale. And because achieving a resource-demand balance maximises profitability, the whole sales process becomes self-funding.

Before we look at ways to grow the business, let's look at the techniques that can help us increase profits with dynamic pricing.

Notes/References

1. Denny, R. (2001).
2. Cohen, H. (1995). *You Can Negotiate Anything: How to Get What You Want*, Carol Publishing.
3. Kennedy, G. (1984). *Everything Is Negotiable: How to Negotiate and Win*, Arrow Books.
4. McKinsey report on deregulated industries, 'The race to the bottom'.

5 MAXIMISING PROFITABILITY

Increasing profitability is all about understanding the nature of the critical limiting resource (that will stop the business from growing eventually) and how the business adds value when it uses it up!

This is all about understanding the price of a bag of beans.[1] Imagine that you owned a coffee plantation. What it is worth depends upon two things:

1. **the amount of coffee it can produce, or the number of bags of beans you can sell. This is governed by the production capacity of the plantation and will vary according to the quality of the crop, the soil, the weather, the harvesting methods and so on.**
2. **what the market is prepared to pay you for a bag of beans. This is influenced by the 'going rate' for coffee beans in the market, but also varied by the qualities of your particular beans and where and how you choose to sell them.**

Your *saleable resource capacity* is the number of beans you have available. Let's say you have 1,000 sacks of beans this year. You can't get any more at short notice because the growing season is over, so this is a *critical resource limitation* on the ability of your business to sell any more even if the demand existed.

You can sell beans in a number of ways and the route to market you choose will influence the amount of profit you can make from the 1,000 sacks you have. You could:

- **sell sacks of beans on the commodity market. You might get £10 per bag according to the market price that will be driven by the laws of supply and demand.**
- **spend £2 on processing and £2 on packaging and marketing per bag to make the beans into ready-to-use ground coffee and you might get £50 a bag.**
- **spend £4 on processing and £3 on packaging and marketing to produce instant coffee and you might get £100 a bag.**
- **serve the coffee as a beverage in a restaurant at £2.50 per cup and you might find yourself getting £1,000 per bag.**
- **serve the same coffee in the middle of the tourist season from a pavement café in St Mark's Square in Venice and a bag of beans is probably worth 1,000 times as much as they were on the commodity market.**

Of course, all sorts of people are involved in the process of growing the beans to delivering a tasty cup of coffee and they are sharing the additional profit that is generated from the value-added price increase at each stage. This profit can be improved by driving down costs if we are clever, or driving up prices if we are cleverer. But the way to transform the fortunes of a business is to move it up the value 'food chain' so that it gets as much profit from its contribution to the supply as possible.

Here's another example of how this might work in practice. Imagine you own a food emporium. You have a stock of 1kg of rare white truffles for which you paid £400 or 40p per gram. You can sell 20 lots of 50 grams at £30 each, totalling £600 and making a profit of £200 in the process. This is 33.3% gross margin (£200/£600) and perfectly respectable on the face of it.

Truffles are hard to source, though, and you won't be able to replace that stock this season. This means that the truffles are a *critical resource limitation* and you have to maximise the profits you can earn from them.

Let's suppose that your normal olive oil sells for £1.95 for 250ml. If you add 10g of truffle, it suddenly becomes highly valued truffle oil that will sell for £19.95 or ten times as much. If you sell 100 bottles at £19.95 each for a total of £1,995, your costs were £595 (£400 for truffles, £195 for oil and assuming the original profit you would have made on the oil was swallowed up by re-packaging and labelling). You make a profit of £1,400.

The process of producing the truffle oil has added *seven times* as much value to the business (the £1,400 we are making now, as opposed to the £200 we would have made selling unprocessed truffles).

The process of being able to increase the price of something, and therefore the amount of profit, because you have changed it to make it worth more to customers is called *adding value*. And the amount of value added[2] for each unit of the key limiting resource is a uniquely powerful descriptor of the ability of a business to maximise profitability.

In the above example:

- the original value added per truffle gram was 20p
  (£200/ 1,000 grams)
- the improved value added per truffle gram was £1.40
  (£1,400/ 1,000 grams)

Improving the *value added* is critically important for maximising the profitability of a business and has a powerful influence on how we can increase profits by:

- providing a mechanism for quickly assessing the 'worth' of a particular deal, trade or process to a business in terms of profits
- making it easier to adopt a dynamic approach to price setting in response to market forces

Understanding the saleable resource

Understanding the limits of the *saleable resource capacity* of a business (its key constraint) is vital for boosting a company's ability to make money:

1. we can protect ourselves from 'overheating' the organisation by taking on more than we can handle.
2. we can work out how to increase the amount of money we make each time we sell something that consumes some of our key resources – by increasing the amount of *value added* per resource unit.
3. we can improve efficiency by minimising the amount of the key resource used by each transaction – carefully identifying the limits often brings clarity to what really needs to happen to make the business run better.

Doing both 2 and 3 at the same time can have an amazingly positive effect on a business.

People and profitability

People are often the most expensive and volatile resource in most businesses. There's another figure that provides a valuable indication of general company health. It is called *gross value added per employee*.

To calculate it, add:

■ **your pre-tax profits**
■ **depreciation**
■ **total wage bill including National Insurance, pensions and your own salary**

Divide the total by the number of full-time staff employed for the same period (including the full-time equivalent of any part-time staff). The result is the gross value added per employee – in other words, the amount of money being contributed on average by each person the business is employing.

Here is an example of how it works out for Jones Ltd:

Pre-tax profits	£	36,000
Depreciation	£	60,000
Wage bill	£	540,000
Total	£	636,000
No. of employees:		18
GVA/employee	£	35,333

Figure 5.1

Of course, all businesses are different and what constitutes a 'healthy' gross value added will change from industry to industry, but here are some examples:[3]

Industry Characteristics	Low GVA/employee	High GVA/employee
Large numbers of unskilled or semi-skilled staff	£ 5,000	£ 18,000
Retailers, distributors and others reliant on selling stock	£ 15,000	£ 38,000
Heavily invested in plant for skilled workers	£ 20,000	£ 70,000
Knowledge-based business	£ 50,000	£ 120,000

Figure 5.2

So we have yet another indication that Jones Ltd are not looking so good if they are in a knowledge-based business, that is, one that uses intellectual 'muscle' rather than materials, machines and labour (like accountancy firms, management consultants, business advisers and so on).

The benefit of the gross value added calculation is that it is relatively simple and the numbers are easy to get from the accounts. The problem, though, is that it's very generic and doesn't get under the skin of a problem in sufficient detail for us to develop an action plan for improving profitability. What we need is a mechanism that pinpoints *exactly* what the people in the business need to be doing on Monday morning to help grow the profits.

Adding value and break-even

It is when we relate the key resource constraint to the break-even point that things start to get really interesting.

Let us take the earlier examples of Smith Ltd and Jones Ltd. You may remember that they looked like this:

	Smith Ltd		Jones Ltd	
Sales	£ 1,200,000		£ 3,600,000	
Cost of sales	£ 900,000		£ 2,844,000	
Gross profit	£ 300,000	25%	£ 756,000	21%
Overheads	£ 240,000		£ 720,000	
Net profit	£ 60,000		£ 36,000	

Figure 5.3

Jones Ltd weren't doing so well because they had narrow margins and high overheads, leaving them with a dangerously high break-even turnover %:

	Smith Ltd	Jones Ltd
Turnover	£ 1,200,000	£ 3,600,000
Cost of sales	£ 900,000	£ 2,844,000
Gross profit	£ 300,000	£ 756,000
Gross margin %	25.0%	21.0%
Overheads	£ 240,000	£ 720,000
Break-even turnover amount	£ 960,000	£ 3,428,571
Break-even turnover %	80.0%	95.2%

Figure 5.4

Now suppose that Jones Ltd are a contracting company with a capacity of 300 hours per week. This works out at about 15,000 hours per year, calculated as follows:

■ Each employee is paid a salary for 52 weeks of the year. So Jones Ltd are paying for 52 weeks × 40 hours per week, which is 2,080 hours per year.
■ LESS 20 days' paid holiday, which is 160 hours (20 × 8), leaving 1,920 hours (2,080 – 160).
■ LESS 8 Bank Holidays. This amounts to 64 hours, leaving 1,856 hours (1,920 – 64)
■ LESS 5 sick days (because there might be), amounting to 40 hours leaving, 1,816 (1,856 – 40).
■ LESS 40 days of non-productive work, totalling 320 hours because of time spent on training and

other activities. This leaves 1,496 hours per year (1,816 – 320).
- **10 people are employed so that is our 14,960 hours per year (1,496 × 10), or 15,000 in round figures.**

A good sense check at this point is that the business is getting 15,000 hours for 20,800 paid. This is a cost-versus-delivery efficiency ratio of 72%, or to put it another way, 30 hours work sold in every 40-hour week. That might be OK for this firm, but productivity can be as low as 50% in some businesses where the ratio of hours sold compared with hours paid for is worse, such as when a service engineer has to travel between appointments.

Hot tip: work out this efficiency ratio for your own company. It is a critical driving force for improving profits!

Improving profits and growth for Jones Ltd

We know from their accounts that Jones Ltd have overheads of £720,000 per year. We also just worked out that the *critical resource limitation* which constrained sales and profitability was the number of man hours they had to sell, which was 15,000 hours.

This means that Jones Ltd need to earn £48 per man hour for every hour of production that contributes to fulfilling a customer order, just to break even. This figure is called the *break-even value added per hour* and is worked out by dividing the cost of the overheads by the resource capacity: in this case £720,000/15,000 hours. It is an extraordinarily useful and sensitive number:

- **useful because it provides a simple indicator of whether a customer or a particular job is making money or losing it.**

■ sensitive because even small changes in the figure are multiplied by the volume of resources consumed to fulfil the job. So it becomes much more important to get the pricing right on a 5,000-hour job (one third of Jones Ltd's capacity) than a 500-hour job.

If your Critical Resource Limitation is man hours, you should now work out the *break-even value added per hour* for your own business by dividing the cost of your overheads by the quantity of your *critical resource limitation*. This will be a crucial number for planning future profits.

Let's demonstrate the value of this with the data we have from Jones Ltd. But now I am going to replace the *% of resource consumed* with the actual hours of production and add a column for the *actual value added per hour* contributed by each customer. This is calculated by dividing the gross profit by the number of hours.

Here is what it looks like (see table opposite).

Yikes! Have you spotted it?

We know that Jones Ltd needs to get £48 per hour just to break even and customer 'x' is only returning £7.32 per hour! This means that Jones Ltd are effectively subsidising this customer by £40.68 for every hour they work for them. Now how long do you think that Jones Ltd should carry on doing that?

Look carefully and you will spot other customers that Jones Ltd are effectively paying to do work for. We can clarify the picture by sorting this spreadsheet by *value added per hour* in descending order, as shown opposite.

You can now clearly see that if Jones Ltd need £48 per hour just to break even, customers g, t, h, e, l, b, z and x are *costing*

Customers sorted by gross profit (descending)

Customer ID	Sales per Annum	Gross Profit per Annum	Production Hours	Value Added per Hour
p	£ 240,000	£ 84,000	600	£ 140.00
l	£ 300,000	£ 48,000	3,000	£ 16.00
af	£ 134,000	£ 46,900	300	£ 156.33
ab	£ 110,000	£ 33,000	450	£ 73.33
t	£ 224,000	£ 31,360	750	£ 41.81
q	£ 94,000	£ 30,080	300	£ 100.27
w	£ 92,000	£ 27,600	150	£ 184.00
x	£ 392,000	£ 27,440	3,750	£ 7.32
ae	£ 180,000	£ 27,000	450	£ 60.00
m	£ 98,000	£ 26,460	225	£ 117.60
a	£ 100,000	£ 23,000	300	£ 76.67
k	£ 72,000	£ 20,880	150	£ 139.20
v	£ 76,000	£ 19,760	150	£ 131.73
h	£ 200,000	£ 18,000	600	£ 30.00
ag	£ 40,000	£ 15,600	300	£ 52.00
y	£ 56,000	£ 15,120	150	£ 100.80
g	£ 104,000	£ 13,520	300	£ 45.07
n	£ 46,000	£ 13,340	150	£ 88.93
s	£ 72,000	£ 9,360	150	£ 62.40
b	£ 20,000	£ 4,600	300	£ 15.33
z	£ 12,000	£ 3,360	225	£ 14.93
e	£ 5,200	£ 2,912	150	£ 19.41
u	£ 16,000	£ 640	1	£ 636.82
Other examples to total...				
	£ 3,600,000	£ 756,000	15,000	

Customers sorted by value added per hour (descending)

Customer ID	Sales per Annum	Gross Profit per Annum	Production Hours	Value Added per Hour
u	£ 16,000	£ 640	1	£ 636.82
w	£ 92,000	£ 27,600	150	£ 184.00
af	£ 134,000	£ 46,900	300	£ 156.33
p	£ 240,000	£ 84,000	600	£ 140.00
k	£ 72,000	£ 20,880	150	£ 139.20
v	£ 76,000	£ 19,760	150	£ 131.73
m	£ 98,000	£ 26,460	225	£ 117.60
y	£ 56,000	£ 15,120	150	£ 100.80
q	£ 94,000	£ 30,080	300	£ 100.27
n	£ 46,000	£ 13,340	150	£ 88.93
a	£ 100,000	£ 23,000	300	£ 76.67
ab	£ 110,000	£ 33,000	450	£ 73.33
s	£ 72,000	£ 9,360	150	£ 62.40
ae	£ 180,000	£ 27,000	450	£ 60.00
ag	£ 40,000	£ 15,600	300	£ 52.00
g	£ 104,000	£ 13,520	300	£ 45.07
t	£ 224,000	£ 31,360	750	£ 41.81
h	£ 200,000	£ 18,000	600	£ 30.00
e	£ 5,200	£ 2,912	150	£ 19.41
l	£ 300,000	£ 48,000	3,000	£ 16.00
b	£ 20,000	£ 4,600	300	£ 15.33
z	£ 12,000	£ 3,360	225	£ 14.93
x	£ 392,000	£ 27,440	3,750	£ 7.32
Other examples to total...			21.0%	
	£ 3,600,000	£ 756,000		100%

Figure 5.5

money to service. Either their profitability needs to be increased considerably, or they need to be replaced. If I were Jones, I'd get the sales team in for a chat, because we definitely don't want Jones Ltd to grow by increasing business from *these* customers.

Note also the value added per hour for customer 'u'. Even though the gross margin was very low at only 4%, the value added per hour is the highest of all. This is because the job only took one hour to deliver. I mention it because it highlights the fact that the *value added per hour* is much more important than the gross margin % as an indicator of 'good business deals'.

Increasing profits through efficiency

Because customers drive a business, we have looked at maximising profits by being selective: analysing the profitability and choosing to work with those that will be best for the business as described above.

Making sure that only our most profitable customers consume our precious resources is just the first stage in the game. The second is ensuring that our techniques and processes are designed to minimise the drain on those resources as well. This is the other reason for properly directing any innovation in your business: if, instead of inventing new widgets to sell, your boffins can figure out how to make the widgets you are already selling for half of the resources they are currently soaking up, you're going to make much more money. So we should also be looking for ways to boost profitability by minimising delivery and service costs through efficiency improvements,[4] even with established customers.

If we look at one of the less profitable customers on the list, such as 'h', we can see that 600 hours of labour delivers £18,000 of gross profit, which is a *value added per hour* of £30 – well below the break-even recovery point for Jones Ltd. Now the customer may not be prepared to move on pricing, so we could be forced to drop them somehow.

But what if the guys in production can come up with a cunning way to fold the metal instead of welding it, and reduce production time from 600 hours to 350 hours for the same job? The *value added per hour* increases to £51.43 (£18,000/350 hours), which improves matters somewhat – not spectacularly, but at least the job is now making money and not costing it.

The more important thing about this approach is that 250 hours of resources have been released, which creates an opportunity to satisfy another profitable customer that we could not have serviced before. This double-lever effect is the way to bring about the rapid increase in profits that will generate the cash to fuel the growth of the enterprise.

The double-lever effect can also transform the fortunes of a business in trouble. This is a real-life example of what happened when it was applied to a building services company that was turning over £10m a year:

	Operating p&l			
January	-£	120,000	Loss	
February	-£	120,000	Loss	
March	-£	120,000	Loss	
April	-£	120,000	Loss	
May	-£	120,000	Loss	
June	-£	120,000	Loss	Sustained loss making
July	-£	120,000	Loss	Customer review
August	-£	80,000	Loss	Cost reductions
September	-£	11,000	Nearly break-even	Value added efficiency improvements !!!
October	£	149,000	PROFIT	

Figure 5.6

This is a spectacular turnaround achieved in only 120 days. Imagine what can be done for a business that isn't losing money in the first place!

Notes/References

1. Pine, B. Joseph II & Gilmore, J. H. (1999). *The Experience Economy*, Harvard Business School Press.
2. Warnes, B. (1984). *The Genghis Khan Guide to Business*, Osmosis Publications.
3. Newell, C. (2003). *A new way to measure your company's productivity*, Business Link Kent, *www.businesslinkkent.com*.
4. Rust, R. T. & Zahorick, A. J. (1993). 'Customer satisfaction, customer retention and market share', *Journal of Retailing* 69, Summer.

6
IDENTIFYING THE RIGHT CUSTOMERS FOR YOUR BUSINESS

Which customers do we want to nurture and invest the majority of our time, effort and promotional budget in?

The general 80:20 rule says that 80% of profits will come from 20% of customers. So one really useful way to rate customers is by the proportion of business turnover they represent and the *value added per critical resource limitation* of the goods and services they are buying, as described in chapter 5.

To simplify all these numbers into concepts that you can share with your sales and operations teams, I find it helps to classify your customers into categories, using whatever metaphors work for your business.

Here is how it might work for an engineering services company that measures its products and services in terms of *value added per hour*, using the Jones Ltd data.

Lead
Earning less than the break-even value added per hour (£48 in the case of Jones Ltd), these customers are heavy and burdensome.

They may be contributing some gross margin but, because they are using up resources that could be deployed to service more profitable customers: they are holding the business back. There are only two viable responses to discovering you are serving lead customers and they are:

- **either increase the *value added* you are earning from them by getting prices up or costs down**
- **or get rid or those customers**

Of course one way of getting costs down is to decrease the level of service until the amount of value added increases to the point where it becomes acceptable. But these customers quite often go away anyway when you attempt that and it might damage your reputation. Better to make a clean break.

One of the easiest ways of forcing such a break is to increase your prices. Those customers who are truly price sensitive will take their (low-margin!) business away from you and give it to your competitors.

Of course you might find that they put up with the price increase and stay with you. As we said earlier many firms have found that increasing prices by 5% will only cause them to lose 21% of their custom so it is worth trying.

Bronze

Bronze customers are earning more than the break-even value added per hour, but less than the ideal break-even point for a sustainable business. Jones Ltd should be set up more like Smith Ltd with a break-even turnover point of at least 80% as described in chapter 2. Bronze customers, then, would be in the *value added per hour* range of £48 to £60 (£48/80%). These would be Jones

Ltd customers 'ae' and 'ag' back in Figure 5.5 and the company should be working to improve the value added per hour, or at the very least ensure that it doesn't fall any further due to discounting, inefficiency or other circumstances.

Silver

Silver customers are what we expect to be 'normal' for the market. In the case of Jones Ltd, this is between £60 and £100 *value added per hour*.

Gold

Gold customers are those that bring excellent profitability in *value added per hour* terms. For Jones Ltd, this is between £100 and £150 of *value added per hour* and they should be looking for as much of it as they can get.

Platinum

Platinum is rare and precious and representative of those relatively few customers that bring exceptional profitability. In our example, they're those earning more than £150 *value added per hour*.

Relative importance

So we can define customers according to their tendency to generate *value added* across ranges as summarised here:

Product/Services Value Added Per Hour

Rating		Description	Value added per hour	Comment
Best	1	Platinum	>£150	Nice work if we can get it
	2	Gold	£100–£150	Really good jobs
	3	Silver	£60–£100	Target profitability
	4	Bronze	£48–£60	Sustainable but unsafe if there is too much of it
Worst	5	Lead	<£48	Break even and below

Figure 6.1

But customers also vary in their importance because of the volume of trade they generate. For us, this means the proportion of resources they consume to fulfil their orders:

	Rating	Proportion of resources	Customers' Trading Volume
Key customers	A	10%–20%	Great if right Value Added – but dangerous customer concentration if >20% and limiting profitability if Value Added too low.
Important customers	B	5%–10%	
Less important	C	2%–5%	
	D	1%–2%	
	E	<1%	

Figure 6.2

And we can combine these two measures to get an impression of the relative importance of each customer:

			Customers/Volume				
			High			Low	
			2%–5%	5%–10%	2%–5%	1%–2%	1%
Products/Services value added	Best	Platinum					
		Gold					
		Silver					
	Worst	Bronze					
		Lead	◄——— Danger ———►			◄— Not good —►	

Figure 6.3

Customers to shed?

Well, maybe! Customers and prospects in that dark sector with a low value-added rating are not good for the health of the business. Basically, they cost *us* money.

However, it is accepted that in many businesses we trade with customers on impossibly thin or sometimes even negative margins for a number of reasons. Sometimes it is because we don't realise it (which is a dreadful state of affairs and requires a discussion with the relevant sales personnel and the accounts team!). At other times a 'loss-leader' approach, where we sell something at less than cost price, is appropriate because it will soak up unused production capacity or bring in more lucrative business later. This is OK if you are convinced that it will work, but remember the many occasions when the big, juicy order that was bound to come on the back it, never materialised. Your customers are aware of such tactics and so are your competitors!

The trick is to ensure that any minimal margin work, which is certain to happen from time to time, is strictly limited in terms of the resources it consumes and the proportion of turnover it represents. That way, the contribution from other, more profitable sales will lessen the impact on overall profitability and should still enable you to pay the bills at the end of the month.

The really dark area on this grid indicates where a significant proportion of the organisation's resources are being given up to low-margin work. This is highly dangerous, because the key resources are denied to more profitable work, and you can quickly reach the situation where it is impossible to pay the overheads on the limited remaining resources at margins that the market will stand. Disaster looms.

If you find yourself in this position, you have two options: raise prices so that these customers either become profitable; or walk away from them. They are killing the ability of your business to survive. Use any means to get profitability up or get out and away – and do it quickly!

Customers to develop

The customers in the shaded sector are opportunities ripe for development. Clearly a strategy is needed that will increase the frequency and amount of each purchase, but for the customers at a 'Bronze' value-added rating, we need also to concentrate on tactics that increase the value added they bring.

Don't forget that the important implication of designing your business around the Critical Resource Limitation is that a 'Lead' customer may be consuming resources that deny us the opportunity to sell to a 'Platinum' customer where we could make much more money!

Designing a profitable business

This has all been leading up to the point which will help to focus the direction the sales activity we need to be engaging in, and that is a design, or blueprint, for the business.

Simply hoping that things will sort themselves out is not a strategy for boosting sales. We know that we might find some 'Platinum' customers occasionally, but it is futile to design the business around them: not only are they rare, but everyone else is looking for them too. We also know that Lead customers are going to happen, either by accident, bad luck or design (if we are running a loss-leader promotion, say). The important thing is to make sure that we don't devote so much of our resources to them that we can't pay the bills.

In Figure 6.4, you can easily understand now why Jones Ltd are so vulnerable; they have too much 'Lead' in their existing customer base and it is dragging them down (see table on next page).

Customers sorted by value added (descending)

Customer ID	Sales per Annum	Gross Profit per Annum	Production Hours	Value Added per Hour	
u	£ 16,000	£ 640	1	£ 636.82	
w	£ 92,000	£ 27,600	150	£ 184.00	
j	£ 100,000	£ 26,000	150	£ 173.33	Platinum
ah	£ 60,000	£ 12,600	75	£ 168.00	691 hours
af	£ 134,000	£ 46,900	300	£ 156.33	
d	£ 4,800	£ 2,304	15	£ 153.60	
p	£ 240,000	£ 84,000	600	£ 140.00	
k	£ 72,000	£ 20,880	150	£ 139.20	
aj	£ 51,000	£ 10,200	75	£ 136.00	
v	£ 76,000	£ 19,760	150	£ 131.73	
ac	£ 68,000	£ 19,720	150	£ 131.47	
ai	£ 150,000	£ 19,500	150	£ 130.00	Gold
f	£ 12,000	£ 1,800	15	£ 120.00	2,520
m	£ 98,000	£ 26,460	225	£ 117.60	hours
ad	£ 88,000	£ 33,440	300	£ 111.47	
r	£ 76,000	£ 11,400	105	£ 108.57	
i	£ 88,000	£ 15,840	150	£ 105.60	
y	£ 56,000	£ 15,120	150	£ 100.80	
q	£ 94,000	£ 30,080	300	£ 100.27	
n	£ 46,000	£ 13,340	150	£ 88.93	
o	£ 116,000	£ 30,160	375	£ 80.43	
c	£ 3,000	£ 1,200	15	£ 80.00	Silver
a	£ 100,000	£ 23,000	300	£ 76.67	1,890
aa	£ 100,000	£ 34,000	450	£ 75.56	hours
ab	£ 110,000	£ 33,000	450	£ 73.33	
s	£ 72,000	£ 9,360	150	£ 62.40	
ae	£ 180,000	£ 27,000	450	£ 60.00	Bronze
ag	£ 40,000	£ 15,600	300	£ 52.00	750 hours
g	£ 104,000	£ 13,520	300	£ 45.07	
t	£ 224,000	£ 31,360	750	£ 41.81	
h	£ 200,000	£ 18,000	600	£ 30.00	Lead
e	£ 5,200	£ 2,912	150	£ 19.41	9,075
l	£ 300,000	£ 48,000	3,000	£ 16.00	hours
b	£ 20,000	£ 4,600	300	£ 15.33	
z	£ 12,000	£ 3,360	225	£ 14.93	
x	£ 392,000	£ 27,440	3,750	£ 7.32	
	£ 3,600,000	£ 760,096	14,926	£ 50.92	Average

Figure 6.4

Here is a design for Jones Ltd that will make them a much healthier company if they concentrate their sales and pricing efforts on delivering it.

Customer or Job Classification	Resource %	Resouce Hours	Value Added per Hour Range	Target Average Value Added per Hour	Target Gross Profit Contribution
Diamonds	10%	1,500	>£150.00	£160.00	£ 240,000
Gold	20%	3,000	£100.00-£150.00	£125.00	£ 375,000
Silver	40%	6,000	£60.00-£100.00	£80.00	£ 480,000
Bronze	20%	3,000	£48.00-£60.00	£54.00	£ 162,000
Lead	10%	1,500	<£48.00	£30.00	£ 45,000
		15,000			£ 1,302,000

Figure 6.5

If 'Platinums' just happen, usually by accident of opportunity, and Lead by pressure of commercial circumstances, then it is Bronze, Silver and Gold customers that Jones Ltd should be looking for in the proportions indicated.

This sets up a policy for sales. The business needs to be allocating a certain proportion of its resources to each classification of customer profitability to be healthy and profitable.

Of course we would like all of our customers to be 'Platinum' and 'Gold', but that's unlikely. The practical approach is to set up the sales process so that it stands the best chance of finding the 'right kind of customers'. All sales activity should be focused on replacing Lead with Silver and that will mean shedding, or improving the profitability of, some customers and winning new ones.

So how can we set the Jones Ltd sales team a target that will deliver this design for their business?

- **We know that their current gross profit is £760,000 and we want to improve this to £1,302,500; an increase of £542,000.**

- If we want to bring in more Silver business, the average *value added per hour* we need to achieve is £80. This means that we need to 'sell' 6,775 hours of goods and services (£542,000/ £80).
- If we sort the data again, this time by 'production hours', then by 'value added per hour', we can see that the largest number of customer jobs committed Jones Ltd to between 150 and 300 hours of work, so let's say the average order size is 225 hours. Notice also that a large proportion of these jobs are in the Gold range of profitability, which is interesting because it could represent the 'sweet spot' for the business – that is, the job that will make them more money. Jones Ltd could do much better than planned if they concentrate on winning more work from these customers.
- Now if we need to 'sell' 5,750 hours of goods and services and the average customer/ job in the 'sweet spot' is 225 hours, the number of new orders required is about 25.

So now we can direct all our promotional activity on getting a new order about once every fortnight. How clear is that? The sales team is ready to go . . .

'But wait!', I hear you cry. 'Jones Ltd is already working up to their limit, which is 15,000 hours. How can they possibly deliver on another 6,775 if the sales team come through with the goods?' This is absolutely the right question to ask if you are thinking the value-added way.

The answer is to gradually replace customers 'x' and 'l'. This will release 6,750 hours of capacity, allowing Jones Ltd to do the more profitable work. The other great benefit of continually seeking customers in this way is that the business's risk exposure is reduced: no *one* customer is responsible for the company's survival.

That's how to grow on a shoestring!

Customers sorted by production hrs & value added

Customer ID	Sales per Annum	Gross Profit per Annum	Production Hours	Value Added per Hour
x	£ 392,000	£ 27,440	3,750	£ 7.32
l	£ 300,000	£ 48,000	3,000	£ 16.00
t	£ 224,000	£ 31,360	750	£ 41.81
p	£ 240,000	£ 84,000	600	£ 140.00
h	£ 200,000	£ 18,000	600	£ 30.00
aa	£ 100,000	£ 34,000	450	£ 75.56
ab	£ 110,000	£ 33,000	450	£ 73.33
ae	£ 180,000	£ 27,000	450	£ 60.00
o	£ 116,000	£ 30,160	375	£ 80.43
af	£ 134,000	£ 46,900	300	£ 156.33
ad	£ 88,000	£ 33,440	300	£ 111.47
q	£ 94,000	£ 30,080	300	£ 100.27
a	£ 100,000	£ 23,000	300	£ 76.67
ag	£ 40,000	£ 15,600	300	£ 52.00
g	£ 104,000	£ 13,520	300	£ 45.07
b	£ 20,000	£ 4,600	300	£ 15.33
m	£ 98,000	£ 26,460	225	£ 117.60
z	£ 12,000	£ 3,360	225	£ 14.93
w	£ 92,000	£ 27,600	150	£ 184.00
j	£ 100,000	£ 26,000	150	£ 173.33
k	£ 72,000	£ 20,880	150	£ 139.20
v	£ 76,000	£ 19,760	150	£ 131.73
ac	£ 68,000	£ 19,720	150	£ 131.47
ai	£ 150,000	£ 19,500	150	£ 130.00
i	£ 88,000	£ 15,840	150	£ 105.60
y	£ 56,000	£ 15,120	150	£ 100.80
n	£ 46,000	£ 13,340	150	£ 88.93
s	£ 72,000	£ 9,360	150	£ 62.40
e	£ 5,200	£ 2,912	150	£ 19.41
r	£ 76,000	£ 11,400	105	£ 108.57
ah	£ 60,000	£ 12,600	75	£ 168.00
aj	£ 51,000	£ 10,200	75	£ 136.00
d	£ 4,800	£ 2,304	15	£ 153.60
f	£ 12,000	£ 1,800	15	£ 120.00
c	£ 3,000	£ 1,200	15	£ 80.00
u	£ 16,000	£ 640	1	£ 636.82
	£ 3,600,000	£ 760,096	14 926	£ 50.92

Figure 6.6

90

Customers deserving attention

In the grid on p. 84, customers in the white squares are clearly providing the greatest contribution of turnover and profits. We need to give these customers all the attention they deserve to maintain and strengthen our relationships with them. The best way to do this is not to sell more products or services to them, but to start asking them some big questions:

- **How are we doing?**
- **What are your further needs?**
- **Can we have some referrals, please?**
- **What are you buying from elsewhere that we could be supplying?**

Asking appropriate questions shows that you care and is a very powerful 'soft sell'. Make sure that you nurture these people, because valuable customers like these, if ignored, will evaporate or be poached! The ultimate aim is to increase the frequency of purchase and increase the amount of each transaction.

There is one possible exception to this intensive nurturing approach. If one customer is delivering more than 20% of the gross profit, then the risk to the company becomes unreasonably high because an accident of fate could result in the loss of that business. A 'maintenance plan' therefore needs to be put into place to keep that customer while more business is encouraged from others.

Adding value

One of the best and easiest ways to do more profitable business with a deserving customer is to *add value* for them based on what they have already purchased. After all, people buy goods and services for the benefits they obtain from them.

Be as specific as you can about the way you plan to do this. If you can quantify the *added value* and show that it's being delivered effectively, you'll have a secure basis for increasing business. For example:

> 'You spent £12,000 on our widgets last year. They reduced your machine down-time by 20%, as a result of which you were able to increase production by the same amount and added £140,000 to your bottom line. Now can I show you our Model B widget which will do the same thing for your other production lines?'

Do you think this customer would give you a hearing? I should say so! First, you've demonstrated that the customer has made a return on investment; secondly, you've shown that you value the relationship by being interested in the customer's needs and delivering on them. The other important thing about this approach is that the price to the customer is demonstrably 'worth it' and this means they're less likely to try and make you reduce the price and give them a bargain – they're already getting one.

Any existing customer will have a 'lifetime value' for a business. This is what they are worth in terms of profits (usually worked out per month or year), multiplied by how long we can keep them buying for. If we work hard to keep customers, they should stay with us for longer and may even become loyal; if they do, the lifetime value will be maximised, not just from the profits generated over the customer's extended lifetime, but also because it costs less to sell to an existing customer.

So what if we have done all that and we are getting as much profitability as we can out of our existing customer base? The thing that every person in business discovers fairly early on is that customers are volatile: they make up their own minds about what they buy and where they buy from and while we may influence this behaviour, we can never control it. The result is that no customer lasts for ever and we shall always need mechanisms for finding new ones. But first we need to be absolutely dear about what our business does for its customers. Read on …

7
BEING CLEAR ABOUT WHAT YOUR BUSINESS DOES

If you are going to set about promoting a business, it needs an identity, often called the *brand.* This requires some hard thinking: only you and your team can come up with the identity of your business, because it's the only way you'll ever 'own' it. The good news is that going about it is a relatively simple and inexpensive process, the key is to be absolutely clear about what your business does for its customers.

Extending the value-added approach is a useful way of developing the very thing that sets your business apart from your competitors: the unique sales proposition (or USP) for your business. It is the most effective basis of competitive position in the market place. It is the things you can do differently for your customers that set you apart and this can be the basis of your position in the market place – or your brand.

The first, and most important thing to remember about developing a brand is that knowing your customers' expectations and needs is an absolute must. You have to be aware of:

- what your customers are thinking
- what they are looking for
- the needs they are trying to satisfy

Secondly, accept that if you are running a small business, your brand is unlikely to drive sales in the same way that training-shoe manufacturers fight for spending power in the school playground. Nor is it likely to have the same impact on international relations as certain drinks manufactures or drugs companies. Nevertheless, it is essential to make your business identity as clearly defined and recognisable as possible.

This is because an effective brand will:

- attract attention
- be memorable
- be instantly recognisable
- increase profits
- ultimately enhance the value of your business

A brand, when it's working properly, drives extra profits to the bottom line.

Brand advertising

This is what *not* to do. For me, the whole area of brand advertising for small businesses is of questionable value. Unless you have huge amounts of money that you are happy to lose, you should avoid the type of brand advertising that is practised by the likes of leading car manufacturers, banks and airlines at all costs. For a small business, it is a complete waste of money.

A brand is not just a name or logo and it is not about just telling people about your business. Think about how many branded logo pens, mouse mats, stress balls, diaries, calendars, key fobs, coffee mugs and other short-lived gimmicks that you have been sent, or picked up and then thrown away over the years. Do you really want to spend valuable time and resources on creating something that won't add value for your business and probably won't even be given a second glance?

There is a school of thought that putting information about your goods and services onto an interactive CD is an innovative way of getting prospects to look at a large amount of information, but I'm not convinced. I have seen too many promotional CDs used as coffee cup coasters. If you do feel that this sort of thing works in your market, then at least make the effort to do two things:

1. **brainstorm to come up with a giveaway that is both useful and memorable**
2. **work out how you can identify which leads, and how many of them, will come from the financial commitment you are going to make doing it**

The one exception to all the questionably useful brand trinkets might be a tasteful calendar. Most people look at their calendar several times a day and if they are subconsciously absorbing your name at the same time, that can only be a good thing.

But, otherwise, the most useful thing you can do is save your money. Because developing a meaningful identity for your business is not going to happen without some thought – it takes a little introspection to understand why a brand is an important foundation for profit growth and promoting the value of your organisation. And that costs nothing.

Simple and difficult

Where the ability of a business to make a good product, do the work to a decent standard or provide a valued service is a basic expectation, your brand provides an identity 'wrapper', or signature, that encompasses everything about you in the mind of the customer. It's different from just being your business name, and brand value doesn't come about from simply having your logo on everything. Correctly crafted, a good brand connects with customers in an emotional way and to people with similar values. This 'meaningful connection' with people is critical, because what you think about your brand is neither here nor there; it is what the customer feels about it that is important. Richard Branson got it absolutely right when he said: 'Your brand is what your customers say about you when you are not there.'

Your brand should be the heart and soul of your business and a template for what you do and how your organisation behaves in every way. In other words, a brand has a personality and that personality is the soul of your organisation.

'A brand is a singular word or proposition that you own in the mind of your prospect. It's as simple and difficult as that.'[1] I think that simple and difficult are the operative words here:

- **simple because it needs to be readily and immediately meaningful to your prospective customers, who generally will not be giving your invitation to do business with them their full attention when they encounter it (most people listen to propositions with a '13-year-old adolescent's mind').[2]**
- **difficult because it can be extraordinarily hard to take your understanding of everything you do as a business and project that into your customers' minds**

in a way that they can extract what is important
for them.

Classic mistakes to avoid

Small businesses make several classic mistakes with respect to
branding. The biggest is that they ignore it, they don't believe that
it is important or they lose sight of its importance amongst the
distractions of everything else.

Ignoring brand value

Keeping your brand in focus is important. Your brand identity is
ultimately the 'hook' upon which you will hang everything else you
do to increase profits and build the value of your organisation
in the future. Although this value may be intangible, when you
eventually come to sell the business itself it can be turned into
hard cash, lots of it, because your brand is the mechanism
that distinguishes you from all similar businesses and makes it
unique.

Ignoring brand promise

The second classic mistake, even where brand value has been
recognised, is that the brand doesn't immediately communicate
what the business actually does.

This often occurs when people can't think of a good name for the
business when they first start up. You can see this a lot in names like
'ABC Controls', which won't mean much to anyone. Alternatively,
some people think it's a good idea to put their own name over the
shop door when they start up. Unfortunately, just about the only
people who care about seeing your name 'in lights' are you and your
mum! Unless your name *already* carries clout in the market, it's not
going to help the business to grow.

So if a baker called Joan Smith wanted to set up in making doughnuts and delivering them by mail order to cake-loving connoisseurs, what should she call the outfit? Here are some ideas:

1. **Joan's**
2. **Joan Smith's**
3. **Joan Smith's Bakery**
4. **Joan Smith's Cakes**
5. **Joan Smith's Patisserie**
6. **Joan Smith's Doughnut Emporium**
7. **Jam Packed Doughnut Delivery**
8. **Doughnut Heaven**
9. **Doughnut Divas**

Assuming that you don't immediately recognise Joan as someone who has already built a worldwide reputation in the field, and you fancied a high-class doughnut, which business name would get your phone call or e-mail enquiry?

For me, it would probably be number 9 because the alliteration works, it's memorable and it speaks to me of the soul of doughnut. You may disagree, which is fine (I quite like number 7 as well because it promises something), but I'm sure you get the idea.

The point is that the identity you choose for your business needs to encompass what you are promising to do for your customers at both a practical and emotional level.

Ignoring brand distinction

If your identity doesn't distinguish you in a memorable way from your competitors or even colleagues in the same fields, you become inseparable from all the other people who do similar things in the minds of customers.

Think of all of the accounting firms in every town in this country. How are they distinguished from one another? How would you find one that could meet the needs of your business? Most legal firms look the same and, for that matter, so do dentists, veterinary surgeons and the dozens of other service providers who put their name on the doorpost and open up shop, full of hope.

The third big mistake, then, is not making your business stand out from the crowd. Many businesses may offer similar things, but they are very different at the core and it is these differences that make them unique and attractive to their customers. By not being distinctive and memorable, a business becomes a 'brown cow in a herd of brown cows'.[3] What you should aim to be is the black-and-white cow in the herd of brown cows that stands out from miles away and promises creamier milk. Or even a purple cow![4]

Making it effective

To be effective, a brand has to be highly focussed and direct, yet different from everything else out there. To build an energising brand, you have to be absolutely secure in your knowledge of:

- **what you are selling (products and services)**
- **who you are selling it to**
- **the need you are meeting (or problem you are solving for customers, which is even more powerful)**
- **how the customer gains tangibly from your product or service**

- the emotional appeal you are delivering on
- the ways in which you are different from the other businesses apparently selling the same thing

A brand identity can also encompass your reputation and a host of other factors such as financial performance, workplace environment, social responsibility, vision and leadership.[5] However, for small businesses, these 'softer' dimensions can confuse the issue and dilute the essence of what a good brand is.

I believe that the best way to think about your brand is that it should:

Represent the promise of what you will deliver for your customers.

Only when you have this is absolutely clear in your mind will you be able to:

- create the brand
- promote the brand to increase sales
- set about 'living the brand' as an organisation

When it works

Getting a brand properly defined, following the above rules, and working well for a small business shouldn't cost too much. This real-life example cost a few beers in a bar and a few hundred pounds for a graphic designer to render the idea. For several years, my own business advisory service was offered under the banner of Gorton Business Management Ltd, which you will agree, broke just about all the rules of a good brand. It was time for a re-think and what we came up with was:

HARD HAT
Business Advice
We build profitable businesses

Figure 7.1

That is a bright yellow hard hat, which sometimes appears on a bright red background with white lettering, and it meets all the above criteria. Does it get attention? Is it distinctive? Is it memorable? Does it make the business instantly recognisable? Does it make a meaningful promise? Is it increasing profits?

I should say so! On its first outing, I actually wore the yellow hat at a networking meeting of soberly suited directors, who all wanted to know why this fool had wandered off a construction site into their meeting. So I explained that my customers are often between a rock and hard place when a hard hat can be very useful, then launched into my well-crafted elevator pitch (see page 105). People were curious and I had a crowd around me for most of the evening.

Three nights later I took a call: 'Were you the fellow in the yellow hard hat? Could you come and see me? My company could use some help.' That meeting turned into a new stream of business!

A week later I was taking the train into central London and working on some papers when the guy in the seat opposite spotted the bright red-and-yellow brochure and asked about it. What transpired was that he was the owner of a distribution business that needed some help. That didn't turn into sales revenue but I have had five referrals from him since. Onwards and upwards!

That's the power of an effective brand. It works when you can make it a meaningful promise as well as distinctive and memorable.

Living the brand

The ultimate test of whether a brand is effective is, of course, whether it is attracting and keeping customers.

The reasons why customers are lost are:[6]

- 1% die
- 3% move away
- 5% move to a friend
- 9% are lost to a competitor
- 14% are dissatisfied with service levels
- 68% believed they were not cared for

Between 65% and 85% of customers who change suppliers are satisfied or very satisfied with their former supplier; it is the lack of care that most frequently destroys customer loyalty.

One of the challenges that follow the development of a successful brand is consistently 'delivering on' it. That earlier idea, that a brand is what your customers are saying about you, is very powerful, because it links what we, as business operators, may want out of a brand with the way that customers are experiencing it.

The process of ensuring that customers' expectations are met is often described as *quality management*. The trouble is, that term has its origins in the technology of making things work. This technical and highly controlled approach, which is certainly necessary in certain industries, somehow denies the passion that is necessary to appeal to 'normal' customers.

'Living the brand' is a philosophy that is more likely to get your customers' loyalty and believing and saying nice things about you. Whatever wins your customers' hearts and minds is going to be a mix of things that are different for every business. Here are some key indicators that focus on serving the customers' needs, to get you thinking about what you should be tracking to make sure your brand lives up to its promise:[7]

- on-time delivery
- lead time – how long does it take to get from order to delivery?
- turnaround time – how long from receipt to repair, say
- time to answer enquiry
- error rate, or number of mistakes made
- profitability per customer
- sales volume per customer
- repeat business per customer
- 'system up'-time, or operating hours versus down-time in a complex system
- response time
- returns and rejects
- unused product
- retention rate
- referral rate
- telephone pick-up response

Techniques for tracking these things include your own data records, complaints records, surveys and so on – I'm sure you can think of others. Once you determine which indicators are right for your business, you can establish the baseline for current performance and set about improving in those critical areas.

As more customers start to experience better value, they'll begin to associate this increased value with your business identity or 'brand' and you *will* start to see the effects of this in improved profits.

The elevator pitch

Once you are absolutely clear about what your business does for its customers, and how to present it, then it is time to think about how to promote it and find those valuable customers that are 'right' for you.

Before you start your promoting and prospecting activities, it's essential to be absolutely clear about what you are selling in terms that are meaningful for the target customer.

The way to arrive at this is to develop your *elevator pitch*. The idea is that by chance, you've stepped into a lift with someone who looks as though they could be a potential customer. They say, 'Hi, what do you do?'. You have only *one* floor to engage their interest and get them to say, 'That sounds interesting, here's my card, will you call me later?'.

The important thing to remember is that when they ask what you do, they don't really care! What they are actually asking is: 'What can you do for me?' Which is an entirely different question, and being able to answer it engagingly is at the heart of successful networking. The key is to focus on the *benefit* you deliver.

Think in terms of what your customer does with your products or services and answer this question as clearly and unequivocally as you can: Why should they buy from you, rather than your competitors?

The answer to that question is what forms the basis of your sales pitch. If it helps, try listing the things you do that help your customers, then list the reasons why they should be doing business with you rather than someone else.

Does that theme sound familiar? If you haven't already done it, go back to Chapter 6 on Identifying the right customers for your business and work on your segmentation to make sure that you understand your customers' needs and motivations to purchase. For our cleaning company, Acme Cleaning, the elevator pitch may look something like this:

> *Hi, I'm Emma from Acme Cleaning. We deliver a responsive cleaning service that guarantees community-housing tenants will have a clean and safe environment they will be proud to live in.*

Notice that there is a structure to creating an effective elevator pitch:

1. **the introduction line (this is me)**
2. **the deliverables (this is what we do)**
3. **the 'so what' line (this is what's in it for you)**

To give another example, my pitch for Jones Ltd could be:

> *Hi, my name is Jim Jones and I help improve production line productivity. We service production line pumps. After forty years in the business we can get spares for any type of pump and can make parts that are not available any more. So our customers maximise profits from their production lines because we minimise the down-time for them.*

Notice how clear and specific the message is. Nowhere is it mentioned that Jones Ltd can also make guard-rails, and do general engineering. That might come out if the conversation develops later. It focuses on what they want to sell *now*. Being clear and specific has two important benefits:

1. if you're in the lift with Jones and are in any way having a problem with production line pumps – or know someone who is – you're going to want to take his card.
2. if you're not interested, you'll want to move on quickly, which sets Jones free to talk to the next person who gets into the lift.

Important things to remember about the elevator pitch are that your goal is not to talk about you but to provoke a conversation. And any conversations that develop from it are intended to build a relationship that will result in a sale, not close a deal there and then. You need to talk about *results*, not products or the company.

By the way, it is fine to have different elevator pitches if you have different products and services, but always choose one to work with on each occasion. Never, ever mix them because it will diminish your clarity of purpose.

Perfect, remember and rehearse your elevator pitch; you'll come to use it time and time again.

Notes/ References

1. Reid, Al
2. Hughes, C. (2006). *Bold Brands Build Business*, Brand ID.
3. Hughes, C. (2006) *Bold Brands Build Business*, Brand ID.
4. Godin, S. (2002) *Purple Cow: Transform your business by being remarkable* Penguin Books.

5. Harris/Shandwick
6. Jones, T. O. & Sasser Jr, W. E. (1995). 'Why satisfied customers defect', *Harvard Business Review*, Nov.
7. Unknown (1999). 'Customer-focused key indicators', TEC Online, www.teconline.com.

8 COMPETING FOR PROFITS

No business exists in isolation. It lives in an environment with things that are helpful and unhelpful: including competitiors.

Marketing is what links customers to business profitability. It deals with what a business needs to do to sell its products and services profitably in the context of its trading environment.

There is a sailing boat analogy that I find very useful to illustrate the way that marketing integrates the components of a successful business. To make any successful voyage you need to take account of five things:

1. **Wind and tide: this represents the external environment of the market you're working and selling in**
2. **The type of the ship: the structure of the company**
3. **Supplies: your assets, including cash, and your company's ability to get more of both as the journey proceeds**
4. **The crew: people and management**
5. **A destination**

Even if you have the best vessel in the fleet – one that's well fitted-out, fully stocked and staffed with a crack crew – the journey will still be hazardous and hard if the wind and tide are against you. On the other hand, if you have chosen your destination so that the wind and tide favour the journey, you can cross an open expanse of water in a fairly leaky boat with people that have never sailed before provided you have enough food and water for the trip.

To stand the best chance of successfully undertaking the journey towards profitable growth, with minimum effort and risk, we need to think about how to approach the journey so that our 'business sail boat' takes advantage of the 'winds and tides' in the market rather than fighting against them.

In 'marketing speak', this is described as *competitive positioning*. In other words, it's about choosing your battleground.

Michael Porter, one of the world's most respected business strategists, argued that businesses can only compete in three ways,[1] which are:

1. **cost leadership**
2. **differentiation**
3. **focus**

David Aaker, another leading strategist, went a little further by suggesting that the ability to make a pre-emptive move in a market was also important.[2]

If you run a small business, I believe the trick is to find a niche and focus on it. Businesses of this size can rarely compete successfully on the basis of focusing on low cost and high volume to attract customers, differentiation (offering something different or unique) or consistently being the first to establish themselves in a particular market.

Let's look at each of these in a little more detail to see if we can determine the best way forward for a small business.

Cost leadership

Many small businesses start out by offering their products at low prices and this can be profitable at first because they have low overheads. It is actually a self-defeating strategy, though. If the business grows, overheads increase to support that growth and quickly reach a point where they cannot be covered by the narrow margin being earned, yet the business is not big enough to reduce costs by means of the economies of scale practised by the big players in the market. This is one of the reasons why so many start-up companies fail within three years – it's known as Death Valley! A pile 'em high, sell 'em cheap strategy is notoriously risky and often leads to business failure.

If you are determined to grow by having the lowest prices so that customers buy from you rather than anyone else, there are two recognised ways of attaining the lowest price position and they are both based on superior experience in the marketplace:

1. **change the structure of the business to reduce or eliminate the running costs (Walmart/Asda do this by having an integrated distribution system and a very effective IT infrastructure to implement it). Other methods include:**

   - **location cost advantage, such as cheaper premises**
   - **government subsidy**
   - **labour cost advantage, through lower-cost workers**
   - **reducing overheads**
   - **economies of scale**
   - **inexpensive capital equipment purchase**

2. **reduce the cost per unit of manufacture. This often presupposes an increase in the quantity of units sold (supermarkets use the leverage of the huge volumes they buy to force down supplier costs). Other ways of doing it include:**

- **no-frills product or service**
- **low-cost product/ design**
- **raw material cost advantage**
- **low-cost distribution**
- **production innovation and automation**

You're potentially leaving yourself open to new problems here, though, as it's all too easy for your competitors to follow with the same techniques. Technologies change and the organisational arrangements or unique supplier relationships you're exploiting to keep costs down won't last for ever. The problem is that however cheap you are, there'll always be another firm that can come along and find a way to do it more cheaply *unless* you work very hard at protecting that position. Even that may not work because the forces in play may be overwhelming – look at the way that low-cost manufacturing in China has affected production businesses in the rest of the world, or how India is influencing the provision of banking and information technology services. You need to keep on top of your game as much as possible.

Differentiation

A differentiation strategy – basically, where your business distinguishes itself from the competition in some way – can work well for a while. For example, your business may concentrate on benefits and service; this is less risky than a lowest-price strategy and could bring greater rewards.

However, unless whatever makes you different can be protected in some way or is inherently difficult to emulate, then competitors will imitate whatever is working successfully. There is also the problem that the basis you have used for differentiation can become less important to buyers.

Do you remember how Volvo used to sell their cars on the basis that they were extremely safe, with impact-protection systems and the like? Subsequently many of the major car brands started to build improved safety into their models until even the original Volvo benchmark was exceeded. Once most of the cars you could buy had reached a similar high safety standard, this ceased to be a motivator for purchase and now everyone just assumes that if they choose a decent model, their car will be reasonably safe.

In business-to-business markets, sophisticated buyers seek to 'level the playing field' with clever buying tactics such as competitive tendering. This is when a specification is written so the every potential supplier can see exactly what the buyer requires. Sometimes the detail is so minute that it effectively removes any difference between competing suppliers' products and services so that their offers can be judged entirely on price.

Differentiation can work well but it needs to be maintained to ensure that it's relevant to your customers and to prevent copycat competitors from intruding on your patch.

Focus

Where a business lacks the resources to compete in a broader market, the best way forward is to focus on one market sector and develop the expertise to serve it very well. In other words, find a niche where what you offer *precisely* meets the needs of that small group of customers who are prepared to pay well for it because it does something valuable for them that they can't find elsewhere. This is an ideal way to create a sustainable competitive advantage.

What we are trying to do is match your business's strengths to those customers who really need or want what you can do well; ideally they will have little alternative choice, other than to buy from you.

The focus approach may include any of the following:

- **focusing the product line**
- **targeting a specific customer sector**
- **concentrating on a limited geographical area**
- **hitting markets where there is little competition**

Aim to claim a sector of the market as your own. If you can dominate it because it is specialised and small, it will be less attractive to competitors.

The problem with this strategy, however, in that a niche, by definition, is limited in its scope for growth. Niche marketing does offer greater profitable growth potential, but also carries a risk of failure because the niche may erode or disappear; it may attract competitors eventually; or it may become overwhelmed by a broader offering that mostly meets the needs. The solution? Build a portfolio of niches to hedge these risks,[3] then aim to dominate them all.

Identifying that niche (or those niches) where we have a definable competitive advantage is one of the most important objectives in boosting sales, because it then becomes an anchor point for all of the subsequent marketing activities.

Segments

When you have a focused approach to marketing, you're able to direct your energies to that small space where they can have most impact on sales. These are called 'segments' and a segment is a group of customers who behave similarly in response to your offer.[4]

What we are trying to do is to find a stream of customers who are looking for something only we can do, then go and stand in front of them with a sign that says we have it.

In technical or business-to-business companies (where one company is trading with another), segments are often mistakenly defined by product types, channels to market, type of industry along with a host of other factors such as country, age and gender and so on. These definitions are ineffective, because they do not describe the way that customers behave and *that's* what you need to know if you're going to sell to them.

It is critically important that you understand what your market segment is and how it behaves because otherwise everything you do to focus on it will be flawed.

There are four classic tests that define a segment:

1. **Is it homogeneous? Are all the customers in that segment driven by the same motivations and needs?**
2. **Is it distinct? Does each segment have distinct needs or do the needs overlap into other segments?**
3. **Is it accessible? Can you communicate with the potential customers in the segment?**
4. **Is it viable? Is the segment big enough and stable enough for your efforts to be productive?**

Finding segments starts with understanding your customers' needs and motivations to purchase.

Ask yourself what is it that the customers in your market are searching for but not getting elsewhere? See if you can make a list of their wants and needs that are not being satisfied by the competition. Then write down a list of what you know you do really well and see if you can get the lists to match.

Against each item on the list, try to find something that makes your business different from the competition – do you offer free delivery, say, or do your staff have better customer-care skills? This process should highlight potential customers for what you do and will enable you to try and identify some special customer needs that only your business can satisfy.

Next, cross out the needs you know exist but which don't really drive buying behaviour (these are often called *hygiene factors*).

Here's an example from a cleaning company that was struggling to win business in the general office cleaning market. When we went through this exercise with them, we realised they could meet a whole series of special requirements for housing associations that their competitors couldn't get anywhere near. Note we have not included things like quality systems and health and safety standards because they are qualifying criteria: they are important for the company to have, because this gets them through the pre-selection process, but don't actually motivate the final choice of supplier.

Housing Association Cleaning Requirements	Acme Cleaning Services	Benefit
Managed service	Committed management supervision	Face-to-face service
Tenant satisfaction	Money-back service guarantee Calling card satisfaction system	

Tenant safety and security	Vetted staff	Freedom from worry
	Uniformed	
	Carry ID	
Rapid response	Reactive mobile team	Fast
Cost of service		Good value
Social agenda		Improving the living
environment		

Internal and external cleaning	Breadth of services	
Graffiti	Graffiti	
Bulk rubbish	Bulk rubbish	
Urination	Hygienic cleansing	
Sharps	Sharps teams	
Vermin	Vermin	One stop to
Lifts	Lifts	remove the
Chutes	Chutes	aggravation
Light bulbs	Light bulbs	
Windows cleaning	Windows cleaning	
Walls washing	Walls washing	
Grounds maintenance	Grounds maintenance	
	Biological hazards specialists	

The next thing to do is eliminate those things the customer wants or needs that you can't actually supply and then scrub out those goods and services that your competitors can provide equally well.

You'll be left with a list of distinguishing motivators for buying behaviour in this group of customers that meet the following criteria:

- **they powerfully drive buying behaviour**
- **they are unconnected – are not different ways of saying the same thing and don't influence each other**

- they are discriminating in that they are not held equally by all customers

An intellectual exercise like this can be very valuable, but there is a better way to do it: rather than playing guessing games with yourself, the best way to sharpen your focus so that you know when you're going to be serving your customers effectively is to ask *them*. Customers are one of your best sources of market information, so why not benefit from all that knowledge? I've found that this approach works:

> *Hi Jane, I have been trying to think of ways in which we might do a better job for our customers. If I bought you a cup of coffee, would you give me 15 minutes to explain how we could improve our service to you?*

It has never failed to result in a really useful conversation, and one of the great spin-off benefits is that most customers are pleased that you care enough to ask.

If you can find at least two distinguishing motivators for your business that drive buying behaviour, and which are unconnected and discriminating, you should be able to identify groups of customers who share similar needs and motivations to purchase. Eliminating clusters that you can't communicate with and those which are too small to be worth the bother will leave you with viable segments where you absolutely understand why your customers will buy the products or services you're offering.

Profit pools

Once you have chosen to focus your selling efforts on a small, carefully defined segment of the available market, you will soon discover that within this segment there will be some areas of business, or products and services that are more profitable than others. These are called *profit pools*. This term was coined in a paper by business consultants Gadiesh and Gilbert[5] of Bain & Co. who observed that:

> *No market has a perfectly even distribution of profit – there are always products, customers, regions or channels that yield above-average returns.*

There are many different sources of profit in an industry and each source will have a different value of profitability. In other words, the patterns of profit generation will often be different from the patterns of *revenue* generation. This may vary by customer, product group, market sector or geography and will result in 'pools' of profit, some of which may be much deeper than others.

Gadiesh and Gilbert tell us that if the objective is to create profitable growth, then it helps to have a map of the profit pools in an industry.[6] By thinking about where and how money is made in some highly competitive sectors, it is easy to understand why so many businesses try to sell you other products while you're buying something from them. For example:

- you're offered a finance deal when you buy a new sofa. This is a great one because it has two selling benefits:

  - it deals with one objection to purchase ('I don't have the money at the moment')
  - the profit on the finance deal may be worth more than the profit on the furniture itself

U-Haul, the American truck rental firm, uses this technique. In a highly competitive market which generally delivers 3% margins, they return 10%. Yet they achieve this by offering the lowest rental prices to their customers. So how do they do it?

They are making each customer more profitable for them by getting an additional profit margin on the sale of accessories – such as insurance, storage space, boxes and packing materials – that are only sold when a truck has been rented. Because they are so effective at doing this, it enables them to extend their scope for improving profits further by driving down supplier costs. (Remember the 'size, fries and pies' upselling technique we talked about earlier? This demonstrates how it works to improve profits as well as turnover.)

Producing a 'map' of the profit pools for an entire industry is tricky[7] and requires a definition of the industry boundaries, estimations size and the way the value chain works. However, trying to figure out where the extra profits come from in *your* business (and that of your competitors and market sector if possible) should be relatively easy, and is a great way of finding out where your customers are price sensitive and where they are not. In other words, you'll see where there is more profitable growth to be had.

In many ways, the major value of your star product or service may not actually lie in its direct profitability. Its main worth may lie in the way that it encourages your customers to buy supplementary products that are even more profitable for your business.

The best profit opportunities will often be found when customers have a need that has been overlooked by, or denied to, competing suppliers. For example, it may be that new product sales have low margins that are driven by the competitive forces;[8] buyer power, competitor rivalry, new entrants, suppliers, substitutes ... whatever, but the major volume of the profit pool is provided by maintenance agreements and accessories.

This sort of information is very helpful because it provides insights into where we should boost our sales effort. So, for example, we may have to maintain our efforts at selling new products (because no-one ever bought a maintenance contract for a product they didn't own!). But any increase in our efforts to boost sales should be directed at the more profitable maintenance and accessories lines.

Such an approach is particularly valuable for a business that cannot hope to diversify much (perhaps because of cost constraints). It has important implications for boosting sales on a shoestring, because it means that our sales efforts should *not be directed at driving up revenue but at achieving* **a larger share of the profit pool attributable to our target market sector**.

One of the best places to start is with our customers, some of whom will be very much more profitable than others. However, it is important to realise that the concentration of profitability in a market sector is unlikely to stand still and the structure of the profit map can change frequently, quickly and dramatically. This is where a small business has the advantage over larger ones because it can move quickly and is one of the major arguments for a dynamic approach to price setting.

Competition

The 'Holy Grail' of competitive positioning is for the business to ply its trade in a sector where there is no price competition for what it does at all. But this is very hard to achieve in practice because a competitor will always emerge where there are profits to be made, so we need to know how to deal with them.

There are two types of competition. There are competitors who are sharing the customers' spending capacity – shall we go on a spring holiday or decorate the lounge? And there are those competitors who are sharing the market for similar products and services.

It is this second type of competition that is of most concern to the small business, because there is little doubt that if you asked business people what is driving their profits down the majority would reply 'the competition', who are 'killing the market', 'don't know what they are doing' or just 'plain stupid'.

The problem is that there's little you can do to control the competition, so don't sweat it! You do have to be aware of it, though. Competition is everywhere and many small business operators fret about what their competitors are doing because of the impact that their actions have on them personally. The trick is to recognise that having competitors is a sure indicator that someone other than you thinks there is gold to be found in the territory you are targeting, and that should be a comfort of sorts.

If it helps, write down all the famous names you can think of and then list their competition: Coca-Cola/Pepsi, Coco Chanel/Paco Rabanne etc. While you're at it, note the ones who are competing on price as opposed to those who are offering something different, or have focused on a narrow area so that they can still charge good prices. That's the way to make money. It's called *exploiting the unique sales proposition*.

It is always better to concentrate on what your customers want rather than what the competition are doing to you.

I once tried sport parachuting and when I had stopped trembling for long enough to listen to him, the jump master taught me a very important lesson. He said: 'Once you are out there, look at the white cross on the ground, because people generally hit what they are staring at.' So those people who look hard and constantly at the competition ... seem to find a lot of it. Look hardest at your customers, you will better understand their wants and needs and find more customers.

This isn't to say that you should completely disregard the activities of the competition: that would be insane, as you need to know how to counter any attack they may make on your customers as well as learning about their weaknesses. But too much focus on what the competitors are up to can lead you to forget that success comes from serving customers' needs better than anyone else, and it is the customer who is best positioned to tell you what those needs are.

Point of difference

One of the things you should do on a practical level is identify points of difference from the competition:

- **What are the competitors' products or services and has your product or service any advantages over the competition that are meaningful and important for the customer?**
- **Why are users of a product or service likely to purchase yours instead of a competitor's and are there any special features that might induce a buyer to get yours rather than that of a competitor?**

The technique for doing this is similar to the one we used for segmenting the market, but this time the attention is on competitors rather than customers.

Competitive tactics

It's always a good idea to have some competitive tactics up your sleeve. When you set out to win more customers, it's inevitable that some of them will already be served by firms who are competing with you.

It's extremely unlikely that head-to-head competition will work. The reason is that the biggest size usually wins if all else is equal. So this is not a suitable tactic for a cash-conscious business!

Other tactics are much more suitable for small businesses, though, and they do work. For example, concentrate on a particular customer where the competitor is weak, perhaps because of a product or service failure. Attack that weakness by offering superior performance, winning the customer, and then retiring from battle for a while. Your competitor may believe that it was their failure that led to the defection rather than your hostile incursion, and refrain from counter-attack. At least if they *do* respond, it may only be to recover the territory they lost.

You could also choose a small customer group or sector where the competitor is not doing so well and make a superior offer there. The idea is to win over a sector that is of no or little interest to the competition. The point about both of these tactics is that you need to pick an area where the competitor is already weak and uninterested!

Alternatively, capture your competitors' resources. If your business operates in an industry where certain skills and relationships are key, such as sales or programming, it may be possible to recruit staff from other businesses, thereby strengthening *your* assets whilst simultaneously weakening your competitors'. Before trying this, think carefully, though; it may not be a good strategy to pursue if you are short of cash because the obvious counter-attack is to offer more money to critical staff to keep them and the costs could spiral.

Stepping back a moment, you'll see that the success of most of these, and other competitive tactics, depends upon cunning insurgence, not head-to-head conflict. What you need to do is apply what little leverage you have to the place where it can bring about the most effect. In other words, exploit a *high force–space ratio*.

Force–space ratio

A high force-space ratio is crucially important, especially if there are some big competing players in your field of operations, because of the 'if all else is equal size usually wins' rule. So focus your selling efforts on a small, carefully defined segment of the available market so that you have a high force-space ratio that gives the best defence against competitor attacks.

If you are looking to boost sales on a shoestring, the implication is that your business has limited resources. The 'focus' approach allows you to concentrate whatever resources you do have on a specific segment of our market[9] as identified above.

Choosing to focus on a small market means that you can do some very important and powerful things that will improve your position with existing customers:

- **build relationships to remove any inclination for customers to defect**
- **improve services levels to remove any excuses for customer defection**
- **create exit barriers that introduce inconvenience for customers who are tempted to defect, such as a termination clause in a contract**
- **build entry barriers to the competition, such as setting up exclusive distribution rights**

Building a strong defensible position with our existing customers means that we can concentrate on selling them more and increasing the profits earned from them. And then we can be very aggressive about concentrating our efforts on those new customers we want to win.

Finding new customers is important, but this can also be problematic and expensive. Let's look at how we might grow the business by finding some new customers. There are two sets of techniques for doing this and they are called *prospecting* and *promoting*.

Prospecting and promoting

Prospecting is about going out to look for new opportunities in an active way, as opposed to waiting for them to arrive.

Promoting the business differs from prospecting because when we are *promoting* the business, we are trying to make as many people as possible aware of what we do in a manner that will attract opportunities to us. A shop needs to attract customers; a business-to-business proposition usually needs to go out and find them.

The approaches are not interchangeable, except on the Internet, where whether something is a prospecting or a promotional technique depends upon how you use it. Before we embark on either of these we ned to be clear about what our business does for its customers, how to present it and our competitive postion in the market place. Read on . . .

Notes/ References

1. Porter, M. E. (1985). *Competitive Advantage: Creating and Sustaining Superior Performance*, The Free Press.
2. Aaker, D. A. (1992). *Developing Business Strategies* (3rd ed), Wiley.
3. Cressey, R. (1999). Centre for Small and Medium-Sized Enterprises, Warwick Business School.
4. Smith, B. (2004). 'Getting motivated', *Marketing Business*, Jan p. 26.
5. Gadiesh. O. and Gilbert. J. L. (1998). 'Profit pools: a fresh look at strategy', *Harvard Business Review*, May–Jun.
6. Gadiesh, O. and Gilbert, J. L. (1998). 'How to map your industry's profit pool', *Harvard Business Review*, May–Jun.
7. Gadiesh, O. and Gilbert, J. L. (1998). 'How to map your industry's profit pool', *Harvard Business Review*, May–Jun.
8. Porter, M. E. (1985). *Competitive Advantage: Creating and Sustaining Superior Performance*, The Free Press.
9. Skellon, N, (2000). *Corporate Combat: The Art of Market Warfare on the Business Battlefield*, Nicholas Brealey Publishing.

PROSPECTING FOR THE 'RIGHT' CUSTOMER

Having identified our true customer base, what we can do for them and how to present that in the competitive environment – what prospecting techniques are most likely to bring in new customers? There is no right answer to this because every business is different, and that is one of the reasons why quantifying the effectiveness of your prospecting activity is so important.

We're not completely in the dark, though: millions of businesses have been trying to find ways to reach new customers for years and we can draw on some of that experience.

Keys to success

'The key to success in selling is more to do with your prospecting ability than any other skill.'[1]

Attitude

Throughout the prospecting process, the crucial thing to remember is that your attitude is the key to good customer relationships: it is the BIG variable that governs buyer choice when everything seems just about the same.

- Be positive and enthusiastic – banish any negative thoughts you may have.
- Turn difficulties into opportunities.
- Demonstrate interest by going back again and again.
- Cultivate a desire to succeed.
- Believe in yourself and your purpose.

Plan the outcome

After a positive attitude, the next key to getting results is to plan. To be successful, this prospecting activity is going to be dictated by four things.

1. We need to take into account our competitive positioning, which means focusing on those sectors where we can compete to win the most profitable customers.
2. Within our chosen sector, we are looking for the 'right kind of customers', which are the ones who will buy what we are selling at a price that delivers the value-added contribution the business needs.
3. We want to try and sell our existing products and services, which is by far the safest route. After all, it is hard enough trying to find enough new customers anyway without having to invent something new to sell them at the same time!
4. We need specific goals to aim for, so that our prospecting activity can be targeted to give us the best possible return from our tight budget.

Let's see how this would work for Jones Ltd, who are under financial pressure:

They are a high-quality machine shop which repairs production line equipment for major manufacturing companies. They have a couple of very large customers and a number of smaller ones. The workshop is very busy making new guards, panels and bits and pieces that break off of their customers' production machines, but they can't get good prices because the customers are clever at buying and competitors will always undercut them if they put prices up.

However, there is one area where Jones Ltd has a competitive advantage: they understand how to refurbish the important large pumps that are essential to their customers' processes and they have invested in the skills and resources to do this well. Competitors would find it difficult to start doing this work because Jones Ltd has the reputation, expertise and equipment. Jones Ltd can easily get a *value added* of £120 per hour for this work, which is 'gold' business and a big pump takes 150 hours.

Remember that the 'business design' for Jones Ltd was to 'sell' 5,750 hours of goods and services and the average customer/job was 225 hours. This looks like the 'sweet spot' for the business, which is that size of job which is just right for them because it makes the most money. However, we just identified that they can do a 'gold' pump job in 150 hours. The selling target for Jones Ltd, therefore, should be: three pump jobs per month (calculated from 5,750 hours of capacity/150 hours per job/12 months in a year).

What a plan! If they can win this 'gold' work, Jones Ltd will put £690,000 on the bottom line (5,750 hours × £120 *value added per hour*). Even if they only half-succeed an extra one third of a million pounds is not to be sneezed at! (Remember, the beauty of the value-added technique is that you can instantly see the financial effect of decision-making). This approach:

- **focuses on a niche**
- **is valued by customers**
- **plays to one of Jones Ltd's strengths**
- **will mean that competitors will struggle**
- **is in a profit pool and delivers a high *value added per hour* because it is in a profit pool**

Outstanding! (And not an imaginary example either.)

Let's explore the techniques that will help them deliver on their goals...

Multi-thread approach

One of the most common reasons why businesses experience a shortfall of sales is that they use only one or two methods to generate opportunities. This often happens because established methods get ingrained: when the business was first starting out, some orders were won and, because whatever the business did worked *then* (and we all like the familiar), they kept on doing it. In time, one or a combination of three things happens.

1. **The business becomes moderately successful, grows and costs are increased as a result. When that happens, even more orders are necessary to sustain the business and the original methods for generating them can't cope.**
2. **The market shifts, the product or service becomes less attractive, it gets harder to sell and margins fall.**
3. **One or two of the most important customers stop buying for some reason, or even worse, the entire customer pool dries up.**

Using a limited number of methods to find new business is a big mistake: no one or two routes to new opportunities can ever provide the number of prospective customers needed to sustain growth in a business.

This is because customers have a variety of preferred methods for finding new suppliers: some people don't like to use the Internet, some don't read the trade magazines, not everyone attends exhibitions and so on. Statistically, we know that there needs to be a mix of at least eight, and ideally ten, different prospecting and promotional techniques employed.[2]

For example, how many of these prospecting techniques are you using in your business?

- **Direct sales**
- **Direct mail**
- **Telephone prospecting**
- **Networking**
- **Referrals**
- **Internet prospecting (e-mail campaigns)**

Direct selling

One of the things that is often said to me by businesses that want to grow is: 'What we need is a sales team.' Sometimes, if the businesses are well-established, it can be: 'We need to make the sales team more effective.'

In my dream company we had a super team of highly motivated sales people who knew their business and brought a constant stream of profitable orders into the company. Then I woke up!

Highly effective professional sales teams need infrastructures to find them, grow them, nurture them, manage them and retain them. Because of the costs involved, this is normally only possible in medium or larger-scale businesses turning over more than about £10m a year.

In smaller businesses, it is quite often the owner or directors doing the selling and if there is any separate sales function at all, it will be vested in one or two people that the owners trust to be effective.

Sales people

The trouble is that only a small proportion of people who call themselves 'sales professionals' really *are* effective. In 1999, a Harvard study[3] of 100,000 sales people showed that just 4% of sales professionals were selling 94% of goods and services. The study was conducted in the US, but I don't think that the ratio is very different in the UK. I have lost count of the number of promising individuals I have seen employed, all professing a selling track record, only to come to a mutual agreement six months later that 'it's not working out'. The trouble is that's six months' salary down the drain with nothing to show for it — that can hurt a small business.

Training and developing sales people is an expensive and skills-intensive process. Sales teams are costly to recruit and employ, and there is a high risk of getting little return on the expenditure, which is why taking on a sales force is not part of our shoestring strategy. Small businesses do not have the resources to find and recruit the best and may struggle to put together a package that is attractive enough even if or when the right people can be found.

But if your business *does* demand that you employ sales professionals, then you need the right type. Sales folk are often described as falling into two camps, commonly referred to as 'hunters' and 'farmers'.

- Hunters are the people who are highly active in going out to seek new business and bringing it back in. Sometimes they are called rainmakers because of their apparently magical ability to make business 'rain down'. They tend to be focused and assertive but less good at nurturing long-standing accounts.
- Farmers tend to be less good at going out to bring in new business from scratch, but they are excellent at building ongoing relationships and maintaining them to get the most business out of them.

To grow a business, you need to recruit 'hunters' who'll go out and aggressively look for new opportunities in every direction. I've yet to come across a recruitment process that guarantees you'll take on this type of sales person, or improves the odds in any meaningful way and, if the chances are only 4 in 100, it's not surprising. The best way is to filter candidates by proven ability, then select those that fit best with your organisation. After that, operate a 100-day trial. If someone is not showing signs of delivering within that timeframe, it's highly unlikely that he or she ever will.

Success activities

One way to judge how successful a sales person is likely to be is to look at how they are spending their time and direct them accordingly. Frank Furness, who twice qualified as one of the top 0.5% of sales people in the world, puts his success down to the focus he puts on prospecting for new clients and spending more time with them:[4]

	Successful sales people	Poor sales people
Prospecting	25%	10%
Sales presentations	35%	23%
Service	15%	15%
Administration	5%	30%
Travel	10%	20%
Self-improvement	10%	2%

Figure 9.1

They also have personal characteristics that include:

- **not taking 'no' personally, because it moves them on to the next 'yes'**
- **taking 100% responsibility for the results and not blaming other things for any shortfall in performance**
- **above-average desire to succeed (intensely goal-oriented)**
- **not mixing with negative people**
- **high levels of empathy**
- **impeccable honesty (it builds referral business)**
- **above-average willpower and determination**
- **ability to approach strangers**

Faced with that list, it's easy to see why only 4% of sales professionals actually do the business – this is not an easy package of skills and attitudes for a small business to find or afford.

Whether you are employing sales people or doing the selling yourself, this is what needs to be done ...

Direct mail

Direct mail is a good way to get your business's name recognised. The difficulty is that mailings are both expensive and have a very low rate of return *unless* the target list is very carefully researched.

Some people say that following up a mail-shot (unsolicited mailing) with a telephone call can increase response rates by 100–1000%, but this seems to vary according to the industry. Others use direct mail because they prefer the comfort of having prepared the target for a phone call by sending them an e-mail, letter or brochure to warm them up. I find that this makes little difference to the success in most business-to-business situations, and sometimes puts the potential customer on the 'back foot' if they can't remember receiving it. You then waste precious time having to explain what you sent.

There are certainly circumstances where direct mail can work, though. The best way to find out whether it will suit your business's needs is to start off gently by renting or buying a small, carefully selected list and then test with a number of different approaches.

When you are ready to start mailing, bear these tips in mind: they consistently produce results.

- Any letter should be short so that it can be read at a glance, so aim for two or three paragraphs, each made up of two to three lines.
- Don't include reams of product information at this stage; sell the appointment.
- Make the letter direct and pertinent to the target customer.
- Always include a postscript after your signature (for some reason the PS always gets read!).

Try something like this:

> Dear Mrs Quinn
>
> We specialise in refurbishing pumps for the food production industry. We can get spares for any type of pump and can make the parts not available any more.
>
> I would like to meet you for 10 or 15 minutes to explain how our service will minimise the down-time of your production facility and reduce your replacement costs.
>
> I will call in the next few days to see when this might be convenient.
>
> Yours sincerely
>
> Jim Jones
>
> PS We can return a burned-out hot fluid pump to you in three days, as good as new, and guaranteed for a year. If you have an immediate requirement, call me straight away.

If you were Mrs Quinn and had a broken pump anywhere in your facility, would you want to take that call?

Telephone prospecting

Let's face it, hardly anyone likes cold calling. Many people actively dread it and very few of us like to receive cold calls in the middle of a busy day.

One company I work with makes cold calls to set up appointments with the managing directors of small businesses. They have found that it takes 200 calls to get three high-quality appointments.[5] If you've done your research and call only those people you think will be interested in your product or service, you might double this hit ratio to 3%. Even so, it's a chilly prospect to set aside one hour a day to make 20 calls over five days to get just three appointments!

You could pay a telemarketing company to make the calls for you, but I have always found the success rate to be inconsistent. Even if you find a service that works, they tend to go 'off the boil' after a while. It can also be expensive: the costs of an effective service will include the list they are working from as well as telephone time and this can mount up to between £50 and £150 per appointment. If you only close one sale with every six appointments, that could cost you £900 per order.

The sad fact is that cold calling is sometimes necessary and if times are particularly tough, it can seem like the only way to improve things.

Remember that the point of calling is to *arrange an appointment* to meet the person you're talking to, not to sell something there and then. It is almost impossible to sell something over the phone to someone you have never met before because there is no basis for trust. So don't even try. What you are trying to do is set up a brief meeting: because you are often approaching busy people, ask for just ten minutes of their time, which most people can fit into their day. If you ask for an hour, it's highly unlikely anyone will agree to see you, so shoot for ten minutes at the first meeting to establish rapport, credibility and interest. If this goes well, you may be granted more time and a cup of coffee anyway. The main purpose of this first meeting is to get the second longer meeting when a selling proposition might be appropriate if the necessary trust has been established. Always fix the second appointment at the end of this first meeting — if you leave without fixing a time, you'll have to go through the whole telephone-tag scenario again.

Getting down to it

Here are some tips for telephone prospecting and dealing with the apprehension that goes with it.

1. Aim to make some calls every day. Once calling becomes a part of your routine, confidence builds, the fear ebbs and it becomes just another business process. Also try to get into a routine. Set aside the same time each day and stick to it. There are two reasons for this: your own energy levels need to be high and you also need to be able to reach targets when they are available and receptive. With senior executives this can be early or late in the business day (when the person who answers their telephone is not around!). Either side of lunch can be good too.

2. Develop a script and know it well. You need to control the conversation, rather than wondering how to react to what's said next. It's a good idea to know the most common objections and how to respond to them.

3. Plan your calls and work out what you are going to say to each person. Compile a list of your 20 most promising targets and research them *beforehand*. If you research during the time you've set aside for calls, you'll get distracted and the process will eat up more of your time.

4. Think about: the target, their company and ways to engage interest; any previous contact activity; your product knowledge, unique selling points and why you are better than the competition; market trends.

5. Get organised and focused. Make sure your desk is tidy. Have in front of you a clean list of targets, a pen, script prompts, your diary and whatever paperwork you need to record the results and any follow-up actions. To help you focus, clear away any distractions and find a quiet place to call. If you run your business

from your home, make sure that pets, children or any other domestic noises don't form the background for your call. To keep up the momentum, set yourself mini-targets such as 'five calls in the next 15 minutes'.

6. Get over fear of rejection. It's energy-sapping and futile. The worst that is going to happen is you might hear a rude word or two, and this almost never happens.

7. Generate a positive mental attitude. Be enthusiastic: sound upbeat. The more positive you are, the more persuasive you'll sound to others. Stand up to make the calls if it helps you focus better and concentrate on the positive results you get, not the knock-backs.

8. Analyse your ratios such as number of calls per hour, number of calls that reached their target, number of calls that resulted in appointments and so on. The point is that you want to understand these numbers for your business and methods so that you can plan to improve. Even if you are working from a computer database, a written record can be helpful. Here is an example:

Date:

Contact	In	Out	Purpose	Result	Next action

Figure 9.2

9. Pick up the phone! Actually making a few calls is the quickest way to build confidence. Stop distracting yourself with e-mails, filing, research and making cups of coffee. Get a glass of water and go for it!

For more ideas about approaches to making those difficult calls and some sample scripts, check out the many free Internet resources available.[6]

Telephone prospecting can be effective. Cold calling is hard work; warm calling (where you have an introduction) is easier, but best of all, avoid the need to make cold calls altogether . . .

Networking

In 1984, a *New York Times* survey on social anxiety[7] placed walking into a roomful of strangers and public speaking in the top two places. Death was third! Many of us think that networking is even worse than cold calling. For people who are not naturally gregarious it is genuinely nerve-wracking to have to enter a room of complete strangers and be obliged to make small talk.

But according to the Chartered Institute of Marketing, networking is the best way of forging the word-of-mouth reputation that brings sales through the door.[8] Many successful business people have one characteristic in common — they get out there and meet everyone who might be remotely interested in buying something. This can be very time-consuming, but in the early days of your business you have more time than you have money, and many networking opportunities take place outside the business day anyway.

Here are a few tips that definitely make things easier and more effective.

Prepare well

1. **Ask the event organisers to send you a list of attendees before the event, if at all possible. Then study the form and identify those targets you really want to meet. If you can get their contact details, so much the better because it can be really powerful to**

get in touch beforehand and agree to meet on
the day.

2. Set an objective. Determine to meet, say, six contacts
   that you can follow up later.

3. Take a discreet notepad and lots of business cards.
   Make sure the design of the card allows people to
   write on the back of them. People who are interested
   in you will want to note down why.

4. Dress the part. Your personal presentation needs to
   represent you positively and authoritatively. Also
   make sure your breath is fresh and that you are
   well-groomed, because you are going to be having
   conversations with many people in close proximity and
   you want them concentrating on your message, not
   keeping their distance!

5. Practise the art of conversation. This means
   being interested rather than being interesting.
   Listen carefully to what other people are saying
   to you.

6. Arrive early. Being ahead of the pack means that you
   get to meet the organisers, get a feel for the room and
   get to see the arrivals. Psychologically you will feel
   much more in control.

7. Affix your name to the right-hand side of your jacket,
   shirt or blouse. This makes it easy to glance at when
   shaking hands.

8. Walk into the room with confidence. Think of entering
   the room as if going on stage: you're not suffering
   from stage fright, but demonstrating lots of
   performance energy! You are there to strut your stuff
   and strut it you should.

When on stage

If you are attending with colleagues or meet people you know, don't cluster in a group and spend all your time with them. It may feel more comfortable but that is not what you are there for. Remember, you are not there to sell but to create rapport, trust and establish a relationship that will allow you to follow up later.

1. **If you want to join a group already in conversation, try this 'butt-in' technique:**

   ■ Listen for a while.
   ■ Join in by addressing the last speaker. Be tactful, though, and wait for an appropriate time to join in.

2. **Don't be shy about initiating a conversation; it's the reason you are there. The easiest way is to pick someone standing on their own and start by making an observation.**

3. **Ask a question: it can be anything relevant and appropriate that will help to ease tension levels. Magic phrases include: 'Tell me about yourself' and 'What do you do?' These are great openers but getting to the 'meat' of whether there is an opportunity in front of you requires something that will bring out a more informative answer such as:**

   ■ Who do you use for. . .?
   ■ What do you think of them. . .?
   ■ What would it take to change. . .?
   ■ How did you come to find yourself in your profession/ doing this job/ working for your company?

- What advice would you give anyone starting out in your profession?
- What separates your company from its competition?
- What is the biggest success of your business this year?
- What's the best thing about working for your firm?
- What are the obvious trends in your industry?
- How would I recognise a business opportunity for you?

4. I'm sure you get the general drift. Experienced networkers will ask *you* some of the questions above, so make sure you have a clear and useful answer ready.

- Now may be the time for that perfected and well-rehearsed 'elevator pitch'. If it is working correctly, it should instantly engage anyone remotely interested in what you do. If this is the case, expand a little.
- Remember the objective: it is not to sell something there and then, but to get an opportunity to call them later, with a view to setting up a meeting.
- Reveal something about yourself: it helps build rapport and trust.

5. Don't talk too much. Express interest in what other people say and do: the most important part of establishing a relationship is the way that you listen. When you're networking, it's tempting to focus solely

on what you do, but this can be a complete turn-off. Make sure you allow people at least as much time to tell you about themselves as the time you spend talking to them. This is important for three reasons: it makes them feel good about their business; it gives you a chance to modify your approach to suit their needs if you need to; it helps you qualify the importance of the opportunity.

6. Give them information that they'll find useful. Perhaps introduce them to someone they would like to know.

7. Create a positive memory; be the first person to offer a favour to the person you are talking to, such as an introduction to a customer or a supplier.

8. If someone offers you help in a similar way, make sure you return the favour; it helps keep the relationship alive. Always thank people for any help you get.

The breakaway

People who are *not* interested in what you do actually give you an opportunity to break off and meet someone that *does* need your deal. I like to use one of these two exit routes:

1. if the conversation was warm and friendly try: 'I can see why you might not have any need for my products/ services, but do you know anybody that might?' Remember that you have not only been speaking to the prospect in front of you, but also to their contact network.

2. or if you feel it would be better to cut away completely, try: 'I can see why you might not have any

need for my products/ services. Let's try talking to some other people, shall we?'

Business cards

Offer your business card at the end of each encounter as appropriate – it helps to bring about a comfortable closure.

One of your primary purposes for attending a networking meeting is to collect and disseminate as many business cards as possible. Wherever you are, accept a business card with grace: it's an important and valued item. This is a great opportunity to comment about the other person's business, logo, what they do and so on. When you get a moment in private annotate the back of the card with something that will remind you of the person and where you met them.

Most importantly, ask everyone who offers you their card if you may have their permission to send out your newsletter or electronic magazine. This is a great way to build up a permission marketing list. (Never be tempted to send out an unsolicited e-mail: this is spamming.)

Networking is also about never switching off. Always carry business cards and be prepared to try and 'click', even at social events. A great way to start a relationship is to ask for some innocent advice in a non-intrusive way then follow up with an e-mail.

Create a system for following up

Don't waste all your hard work. As soon as you're back in the office, rank the targets you've met in order of potential opportunity, record their details using whatever system suits you best, and then get in touch.

You should always follow up leads with a phone call or e-mail. The approach should be along the lines of: 'So glad to have met you last night and I would like to continue the conversation . . .'

Plan to re-connect with at least four people every day with some kind of help or offer, not a sales pitch. What you are trying to do is build the biggest network of contacts possible and keep it alive. In time your network will develop into a hierarchy of relationships that will look something like this:

Acknowledged contact

Understanding

Acceptance

Respect

Trust

Rapport

Bond

It takes time and patience to get results, so don't give up early. Keep plugging away and you'll get the results you want. You'll build a large network quickly if you make sure you speak to at least one person you *don't* know at every event. Also try to attend networking events regularly; it's the best way to keep up momentum and get the most out of them.

In your search for new contacts, you'll find that the greater the mix within a network, the better. 'Open' networks which have a wide and varied proportion of individuals from different industries and backgrounds, are much more useful than 'closed' networks (such as trade associations) because there are more opportunities to connect with different people.

Virtual networking

The Internet is opening up a range of possibilities for virtual networking. These cost little or nothing, so they qualify for our shoestring approach, but because of the sheer volume of possible contacts it can be hard work and tough to get genuine leads. It can also take time to see results, but it's definitely an option to try out for your business (see Chapter 12).

Check out portals like *www.linkedin.com* and *www.ecademy.com*.

Referrals

There is a school of thought that we are only six steps away from the opportunity to speak to anyone we wish to target. The antidote to cold calling is getting referrals. This is the 'silver bullet' of marketing and by far the cheapest and most effective method of prospecting for a business on a tight budget.

Referrals are powerful introductions to potential customers because they're based on your having done a good job for a customer and developed a good working relationship with them. Referrals are *only* given if a customer is pleased and as a favour for the recipient. Also, if you have been referred to someone, that person is probably already predisposed to want to talk to you. After all, their friend would only send them someone good, wouldn't they?

One of the reasons that referrals are such a powerful prospecting tool is that 'Even those deaf to a salesperson, blind to the claims of brochures and immune to adverts will listen to a friend or to a respected colleague.'[9]

It's essential, therefore, that you have the means to generate, capture and follow up referrals as an integrated process in your prospecting activity. The problem is that customers rarely think of recommending goods and services they've benefited from. It just isn't high on anyone's agenda. Customers may be reluctant to volunteer referrals for a number of reasons:

- **risk. They are afraid of upsetting friends or relatives by causing a stream of unsolicited calls, or worse,**

147

putting a friend in touch with someone who then
doesn't do a very good job.

- **confidentiality.** Many customers feel that what they
  have bought is personal to them.
- **worry.** People may be concerned that their friends will
  think they're giving their details out without
  permission.
- **social standing.** Some customers think that sales
  people are beneath them and customers sometimes
  disqualify their friends from such introductions on the
  basis of their class or income.
- **lack of confidence in the sales person** or whether he or
  she is going to be around for long enough to make any
  sort of investment in the relationship to make it worth
  their while.
- **perceived lack of contacts.** Some customers don't
  think they know anyone worth referring.

If you want to secure some referrals, you'll need to ask for them in
a manner that will overcome these objections. Also bear in mind
that you should be looking to get internal referrals within a large
organisation as well as external referrals.

The other reason why referrals don't often happen is because
business owners are reluctant to ask for them. But if referral
prospecting works so brilliantly and costs so little, why isn't everyone
doing it? There are a host of plausible reasons, including:

- **they're only for unsuccessful people**
- **it's a labour-intensive process**
- **I'm a professional and it makes me look like an
  insurance salesman**

- sounds desperate
- lack of response in the past

If you feel slightly embarrassed about it, get over it: the alternative to getting those names is cold calling, and how much fun is that?

There are several ways to ask for referrals without being embarrassed or causing embarrassment. Here are two of my favourites:

- 'If we had to swap jobs today, who would be the first three people you would call if you were in my shoes?'
- 'I'm glad you're pleased with what we've done for you. Can you think of three colleagues or business associates who could benefit from what we do in the same way?'

It can also help to oil the wheels by referring a useful contact to someone first. You will often find that people respond positively and want to return the favour.

Request specific referrals so that you narrow the customer's focus on what you are asking for. Ask for both the number and type of referrals that will be useful to you. The point is that we want the customer to think about it and dig deep, not just toss you the first name that comes into their heads. So if they give you one name, ask for two more.

If you're meeting someone face-to-face, open a notebook and write everything down. It tells your customers that you value the information, obliges them to be thoughtful about getting the details correct and there is nothing like an open notebook, a poised pen and silence for prompting just one more name. Also:

- get as much information about the referral as possible
- ask for permission to use the customer's name

- ask for help with obtaining an appointment with the referral if you, or they, think you're going to need it
- contact the referral as soon as possible
- inform your customer about the outcome of the contact. If a referral results in some business, send your customer a note and reward them with an appropriate gift, even if it's just a drink at lunchtime, to let them know you value what they did. And when you ask them for some more names in a few months they're going to be happy to help.
- rank referrals as you do customers

The best time to introduce referrals into the conversation

The best time is when your customer has just given you an order. They obviously have confidence in your business, or they wouldn't have committed to buy. But this question is very powerful if you ask it at the right time: 'What do we need to do to ensure that you recommend us?' This tactic:

- deals with any lingering doubts the customer may have which can be eased by letting them know that you want to do your very best for them.
- brings out any special agenda that you may not know about. I once had the reply: 'Well, this is a very important purchase for us. If it goes well, I could get promoted to be manager of the buying department. If it doesn't, I could get fired.' Now how powerful is that?
- sets up your right to ask for referrals if you do a great job.

Multi-level referral system

Referrals work brilliantly when highly motivated and focused sales people are using them as a part of their prospecting toolkit. But the way to *really* get them working for your business is to get the whole company involved.

This ideally needs a properly integrated customer relationship management (CRM) system to get it going properly. These can be expensive and time-consuming to set up and may not be an option for every small business, but for some great ideas about practical referral techniques and integrating them into your company, check out Roy Sheppard's website.[10]

Another important activity is to build 'referral alliances'. These can take many forms, such as networking groups and cultivating key people in the industry. You'll find that most people know a few other people. But you will come across individuals that are astonishingly well-informed and well-connected. These are mavens[11] or centres of influence. Find them and cultivate them.

The most important things to realise about referrals, which are amongst the most powerful and cost-effective prospecting tools, is that they won't happen unless you set out to:

- **generate them**
- **capture them**
- **'process' them by following up**
- **reciprocate by offering referrals of your own**

Dead leads

There's always something to be gained from an opportunity, even if someone doesn't want to buy; a sales lead is never completely pointless if you use unproductive sales leads as a source of referrals. Try something like this:

I can understand why you don't need our service at the moment, do you know of any colleagues that may benefit?

You'll be surprised at how helpful people can be.

Notes/References

1. Furness, F. (2003). *Finding new clients*, Nicholson Smith Publishing.
2. Cardell, C. (2006). www.cardellmedia.co.uk
3. Asher, J. (2002). 'Teach and reinforce the 10 skills of super salespeople', Vistage, www.vistage.com.
4. Furness, F, (2003). *Finding New Clients*, Nicholson Smith Publishing.
5. Milne, S. (2006). *Accreditation Training and Support Manual*, Penman Strategic Ltd.
6. Furness, F. (2003). *Finding New Clients*, Nicholson Smith.
7. 'Social Anxiety' (1984), *New York Times*.
8. Knowledge Hub (2006), Chartered Institute of Marketing, *www.cim.co.uk*.
9. Sheppard, R. (2001). *Rapid Results Referrals*, Centre Publishing and also *Meet, greet and prosper, www.royspeaks.com*
10. Sheppard, R. (2001). *Rapid Results Referrals*, Centre Publishing (*www. royspeaks.com*).
11. Gladwell, M. (2001). *The Tipping Point: How Little Things Can Make a Big Difference*, Abacus.

10 PROMOTING THE BUSINESS

There are a number of different ways of promoting a business to attract new customers. They're all effective in their own ways, but not equally cost-effective, so choose carefully!

We need a multi-thread approach to promoting the business for the same reasons that were important for our prospecting.

To reach the entire population that might be interested in what your business does you also need to be working on several promotions that integrate with the prospecting techniques to make up that minimum of eight ways to generate new business we need. How many of these promotional techniques are you using in your business?

- Radio and TV advertising
- Public relations
- Public speaking
- Joint ventures and strategic alliances
- Shows, exhibitions and other events
- Advertising
- Direct response advertising
- Internet prospecting (website and pay-per-click advertising)

Measure and test

After not using enough techniques to generate new opportunities, another big mistake is that businesses rarely measure and test whatever techniques they are using. As a result, they have no way of knowing how efficiently their promotional expenditure is working for them.

So when times get hard and budgets get cut, most business operators instinctively chop the marketing or promotional budget first. This is because saving money this way has little direct impact that will be felt immediately. Few firms can actually measure the return on their promotional investment, so doubt exists about how effective it really is. That doubt makes it easier for people to rationalise the cost-cutting. Is your company one of these?

Yet almost everything you read about cost-cutting when times get hard suggests that you should leave the marketing promotional budget alone at the very least, or – even better – increase it. The rationale is that increased spending on promotions will maintain or increase sales, and thus enable the firm to trade through the difficulty.

I don't agree with applying this as a blanket rule for two reasons. First, money spent on a promotion will almost certainly be wasted if you cannot tell what results you will get from spending it. Secondly, understanding the reason for a downturn in trade is important. Some products go out of fashion and some businesses experience seasonal or market fluctuations. If people don't want to buy skiing equipment in July, carpets in the week before Christmas or winter coats in August, there's little point in trying to promote them. Any campaign is unlikely to create demand, so the money will be wasted.

If you're on a tight budget but want to promote your business, there are two fundamental rules.

1. Cut immediately any money being spent on branding or adverstising that isn't leading directly to quantifiable sales.
2. Trial any promotional technique in a small-scale, low-cost operation first. If it's a success, you can roll it out later. This rules out TV and radio advertising since it is both expensive *and* large scale.

Only this way can we get to the point where a £1,000 promotional budget is beneficial because it resulted in £100k of new orders worth £10k of margin. When those results are repeatable the next question becomes how often do you want to spend that £1,000?

Later we'll explore which promotional and prospecting techniques we should be investing money, time and effort in. Before we get into that detail, however, it's important to understand that to get the best value for money out of any investment in finding new customers, it is essential to:

1. adopt a multi-thread approach to prospecting for business – because you need at least eight different techniques to cover any market sector
2. measure and test every promotion in terms of money spent and employee time. These expenses must be capable of being compared with the original target group, the opportunities developed, orders converted, value per order and gross margin per order.

What *you* think will get customers clamouring to buy your goods and services is hardly relevant. What matters is what actually gets them to spend, and the only way to find that out is to try different approaches until you find what works best.

155

Done correctly, one of the most powerful things about the multi-thread approach is that each technique reinforces the other and potential customers become aware of our offering from several different directions at once.

Sources of business

Having a basketful of techniques is one thing, but we need to apply them. And for the prospecting techniques in particular, we need to target the people that are most likely to give us business.

So where do we start? Where are we likely to find opportunities that will suit these approaches? Here are a few ideas.

Customers

In your customer portfolio you are going to have:

- **ex-customers**
- **cool customers – where there is hardly any relationship worth speaking of**
- **warm customers**
- **good customers**
- **key accounts or best customers**

They are obviously all worth talking to as potential sources of increased business or new business. It is often particularly interesting to examine why the cool customers are 'chilly' if only to explore ways of improving the relationship to warm them up.

One of the areas often forgotten about is ex-customers. Assuming that they haven't gone away irrevocably because of something nasty your business did to them, keep in touch with past customers, even if they have not bought anything for a while. Even those who are now served by a competitor present an opportunity: your competitors aren't perfect all the time either, and customers deserve a choice.

Stay in touch, find out what they like about what they are getting now and what they don't like. Persistence often pays off.

Brainstorm

Let your mind run free and think about all of those potential customers you have never thought to contact, even if they are not in your industry sector. For example, Jones Ltd could start thinking about all those users of pumps that are out there in different industries, such as water authorities, oil industry, fire service, food processors, distillers, brewers, pharmaceuticals or anyone else that might have a large-scale pumping requirement.

Colleagues, friends and relatives

Talk to people in other non-competing businesses and get their suggestions to add to your own brainstorming activity.

Lists

You can buy lists that contain details of people that have agreed to accept promotions for the products or services you offer. If you are considering this route you *must* make sure that:

- **the people offering the lists for sale are reputable**
- **the information you require is on the list**
- **the list is up to date – anything older than 12 months will have a very high proportion of 'gone-aways'**

Supply chain

Look at the supply chain for gaps that you can fill with your products and services. For example, Jane Ltd might contact firms that manufacture pumps and and want to concentrate on that area, and may be pleased to offload the service problem while ensuring that their customers are well supported.

Networks and referrals

You are allowed to contact the people in the list in the way you want to.

Radio and TV

These options are generally too expensive to even think about if money is scarce, but if you do have a bit of leeway in the budget, they may work wonders.

However, you must be able to measure the relationship between the money you are spending and the return on the investment. Local radio might work for a certain kind of business, but how will you measure its effect? If you are renting air chillers, and sales increase in hot weather anyway, how will you know how much of the increased business was caused by the money you spent on the radio advertisement and how much would have happened just because it was hot?

For such a business I would want to understand the correlation between temperatures, humidity and sales on each day (the historical data would be available from the Meteorological Office and the sales ledger); then I would compare this with what happened shortly after each time the advertisement played. This sounds impractical but the data is readily available and this kind of thing is worth doing, otherwise you are spending money and don't know what you are getting for it.

Radio and TV advertising can be high risk because it's very difficult to test it on a small scale at low cost. You should hesitate before investing in radio and TV advertising unless it's money you can afford to lose.

The exception to this is when you can get the exposure for free. Some local radio stations are always looking to interview interesting people with a message that is of current interest. This can be a great way to build your profile quickly provided you prepare and present well.

Public relations

Public relations, or PR, is much better than advertising: if you've positioned yourself as an expert in your industry, you get more 'credit' for editorials since they are seen as more authoritative than paid-for advertising.

There are agencies that specialise in developing the public profile for larger businesses. For a small business, though, the important thing is just to 'get out there' for the minimum cost and the great thing about PR is that it can be free. (Yes, you can get free media coverage for your business in newspapers, magazines and even radio and TV.)

The power of PR comes from positioning yourself as an expert and making yourself available to a news-hungry media. This isn't about academic qualifications, but the fact that to the majority of editors and readers, you're an expert in your line of work. Decide what your field of expertise is and promote yourself accordingly. You have knowledge and experience that the media needs to hear about.

Start with a one-page press release sent to a targeted media group; later on you might consider feature articles. Make it as easy as possible for the editor just to pick it up and publish it in the next edition. While you are at it, find out the future copy deadlines that will enable you to prepare a little something for each future edition, which may be very gratefully received by a hard-pressed editor looking to fill a gap.

Be warned that the first thing that is going to happen after your article is accepted for publication is that the journal's advertising sales people will call and try to sell you some column inches of advertising space. They can be very persuasive. I find that it helps to explain that you want to see the response to the editorial before investing in advertising.

Resist for now, you don't need both. Also check out the section on advertising later in this chapter.

Public speaking

Public speaking can be an extension of your public relations programme, or it can be more specific and targeted. Like networking, public speaking is scarier than death for some people. But if you aspire to being a big hitter in the world of business you need to build skills and confidence. Most people find that giving seminars is highly productive, saves time and is fun – once you remember what the actors tell us; it's not stage fright but performance energy!

Find out which groups contain your potential customers. Many organisations are meeting regularly and need to spice up these meetings with outside speakers.

Don't base your presentation on a sales pitch, though. What you need to do is deliver something that is useful and valuable for your audience. Find out what you can contribute for them. Start by telling them the three things they will learn about during your presentation and then summarise what you've told them in a memorable way, so that they can take some knowledge away that is of benefit to them. It's only once you've built rapport with the audience and delivered something of value that you've earned the right to give them your sales pitch (in other words, a brief summary of what your business can do for them).

Arranging speaking engagements is the same as setting up any kind of meeting: target ten organisations and aim to book two speaking engagements from those calls or letters. There is sometimes a cost for this activity because many organisations would like your business to put some sponsorship money on the table; even if they are charging an attendance fee, it rarely covers the cost of an event.

Paying the costs of an event is fine *if* you can measure the return; one firm of accountants I work with reckons that they get at least two opportunities resulting in one new client out of every seminar, and the lifetime value of a client to an accountant makes it well worth doing.

Here are some tips for communicating with impact.

1. **Prepare carefully. This includes checking out the environment and equipment you will be using.**
2. **Rehearse your presentation in front of a trusted friend, colleague or family member who can give you honest, constructive feedback.**
3. **Research your audience to the point where you know what they are looking for out of the event and can connect with them.**
4. **Kick off with a big start to engage attention (you may have to work up to this if you're a relative beginner!).**
5. **Most novice presenters are thinking so hard about what they are saying when they are 'on stage' that they forget the manner in which they are saying it. Think about how you are delivering your message and what the audience is experiencing.**
6. **Use appropriate language that helps to reinforce your position as the expert on the subject you are speaking about.**

7. Involve your audience: be interactive and ask questions, which shows you care.
8. Don't do things by halves – business people are fed up with boring presentations and there are real benefits for injecting a bit of showmanship.

Joint ventures and strategic alliances

One of the cheapest ways to promote a business is to come to reciprocal arrangements with other businesses working in the same sector but not competing. Such joint ventures and strategic alliances can be very useful because the other businesses you encounter may have access to customers you need. If you can figure out something that's in it for them, they may steer customers your way. The 'what's in it for them' angle is important, because people forget to do favours when they get busy. So any distraction has a cost and needs to be rewarded with a commission.

Look out for non-competing businesses who already have customers you want to reach and find a win-win for both partners. If *you* have a strong customer base, you might also think about a joint venture the other way; it could be lucrative.

For example, one limousine taxi service I know advertises and places their cards in a ladies hairdressing salon. The logic is that a high proportion of these customers are preparing for a special event and it might be nice to arrive in style. This didn't work well until the first introduction resulted in 10% of the fare being paid as a commission to the salon. Things then picked up very quickly because the salon benefited directly and indirectly from offering the service to their customers. The limo firm is absolutely scrupulous about making fair payments to the salon with a note of who the customer was and where they went, because they want the salon to keep working for them. The list is kept by the appointments book in the salon for two reasons:

1. the salon realised that once the customer had the limo card, they might lose out on any future commission. They now offer a limo booking service on behalf of the customer.
2. the salon has a handy record of trips that allows them to greet a customer personally ('Hello Mrs Jones, nice to see you again. How was the show last month?').

It all works beautifully. Do remember, though, that this type of system can only work well if both businesses benefit equally. There must be absolutely no possibility of rivalry between the businesses, either. If there is a clash of any type, it can all get highly complicated (and bad tempered) very quickly.

Shows, exhibitions and other events

These are worth a mention because they can be very effective for some businesses. It is difficult to say whether such events are worth doing because the results seem to vary according to the type of industry and the company itself. The major problem is that these things are never cheap, either in terms of money or work involved. A modest 10m² stand could cost around £3,000, added to which are the costs of dressing and staffing it.

Certainly, well-established companies seem to appear at trade shows year after year. Some have massive stands staffed by several people and clearly no expense is spared. Clearly they think it is worth the effort – but are they really measuring it? Or do they fear the market reaction if they don't turn up one year?

For the small business that is relatively unknown, a budget stand in the far corner of the exhibition hall can be expensive, create a negative impression and attract few opportunities.

Only you can establish whether this will be a worthwhile source of new customers for your business. My recommendation, if you are going to try it, is to start small, concentrate on doing it as well as you can, then measure the results. If it works, by which I mean it brings in more gross profit than you spent, next year invest more and go bigger. Otherwise don't do it again.

Advertising

Advertising has long been perceived to be one of the most effective ways to get a firm's products and services in front of potential customers. Big companies wouldn't spend vast amounts of money on it otherwise. The immense costs come not only from the adverts themselves, but also from all the preparatory work that goes into making sure they're effective. This can include:

- **calculating the budget and return on investment anticipated**
- **working out the target market**
- **finding the most effective way to reach that market**
- **deciding on the best time and place to advertise**
- **creating the message to be conveyed**
- **agreeing the action to be taken by the recipient**

All of which is good stuff that you should certainly be doing if you are advertising to promote your business.

The problem is that for most small or medium-sized businesses, advertising simply *does not work*.[1] I often encounter a situation in medium-sized business where there is a 'marketing budget' of (sometimes) tens of thousands of pounds. This is spent on a variety of activities, such as Yellow Pages, trade magazines, trade shows and so on. When I ask what the business is getting back for its money, the reply is often along the lines of:

- **'We don't know, but it's in the budget and we have to spend it by the end of the year or lose it.' (Eek!)**
- **'We don't know, but if we stop spending it customers won't know about us.' (Okay, but how many customers have you got that arrived via that advertising route? 'Don't know' is the reply in most cases!)**
- **'We don't know, but if we stop spending it our competitors will think we are in trouble and then something bad might happen.' (Yeah, right. If you are operating at 25% margin and spending £50,000 on advertising you need £200,000 in sales to break even, how bad can it get?)**

The point is that if you can't answer *precisely* how many targets your advertising is directed at, how many customers your advertising is bringing in, how much they are spending and the gross margin on those sales, then you are wasting money!

Unless you are a very large business with highly sophisticated methods of relating advertising expenditure to response, (in which case you are reading the wrong book) it's madness.

Direct response advertising

We've established that printed advertising is expensive and even those who swear by it will admit that about half the money is wasted; the problem seems to be identifying which half. However, something that is both expensive and has a 50% wastage rate cannot be part of growing a business on a budget. If something isn't working for you, **stop doing it**. Save the money, and do something more productive with the budget.

The technique you need is called *direct response advertising*. This means spending a very small amount of money on a promotional idea, then testing and measuring to see what works. It directly measures and relates the response of the market in terms of enquiries and sales to the advertising stimulus. You should then compare the value of the response with the cost of the promotion. Only when you can see that £1 spent on an advertisement or promotional campaign brings in many more £s of gross margin have you found a winning formula. If things go well, roll it out on a larger scale. If the original target group was chosen carefully in the first place, then the numbers will hold up and the result will be repeatable.

For this to work, you have to know how each customer heard about your offer. Obviously you can ask customers at the point of purchase and that is sometimes helpful: if they have come through the door at a special event, you can count the opportunities in and the buyers out. But with advertising it gets a little trickier; you need to set up a system so that the response to an advertisement or other promotional activity will tell you where it came from. The classic ways of doing this are along the lines of:

- 'Bring this coupon in for a free doughnut!'
- 'Quote this reference for your promotional discount'

You must track this data because it is the only way you will ever be able to work out what promotions deliver value for money. Ultimately – and even more importantly – it will tell you what causes sales. Test and measure the effect every time you run an advertisement or make a change to one that is already running. It is the only way you will find out what works.

Basic rules

Here are the basic rules for producing an advertisement that have been established by the people who are successful at advertising:[2]

- headlines are the most important thing, because it is the headline the gets the rest of it read
- sell the benefits, benefits, benefits to the reader – don't get fixated on product features
- don't advertise on the left-hand page; it's not as visible as a right-hand one
- never pay the full rate for advertising; there's always a deal to be had
- don't follow what the competition are doing; the 'me too' approach never works as well as your own brand initiative

Notes/ References

1. Cardell C. (2006). *www.cardellmedia.co.uk*
2. Gehl, D, (2006). www.marketingtips.com.

11 PROMOTING AND PROSPECTING ONLINE

The distinctions between prospecting for new opportunities and promoting the business get blurred when you're doing both online. The Internet can tackle these two tasks as well as helping to maintain a relationship with existing customers, suppliers and so on. Technology also makes it much easier for you to track the impact of promotion and prospecting campaigns.

Website

Having a website for your business will have a big impact. Although it will probably only take about 20% of the trade from the traditionally-established buying methods,[1] this is likely to increase in time. Of even more importance is its use as an information resource. Even people who are looking for products that might not be sold online will check out the Internet to see 'what's out there'. Most critically, anyone who was interested in your 'elevator pitch' and has taken your business card will check your website next to find out more about you: see it as a showcase for your business.

Not only must your website act as an online brochure, but to be an effective promotional tool it's increasingly important that it attracts potential customers in its own right. However, this isn't as easy as the electronic equivalent of putting a card in a newsagent's window.

Designing and building a website requires at least six distinctive and separate skills if the website is to be an effective source of potential new business.

1. Branding that produces a clearly defined proposition: we touch upon this in Chapter 7.
2. A designer who can translate that brand identity into something that will encourage people to visit your site and then hold their attention once they're there.
3. A copywriter who knows the power of headlines to grab attention, how to prepare killer sales copy and provoke a response.
4. A positioning tactician who understands how to get the site to the top of the search engines. Search-engine optimisation, as it is called, is important, as you need to get ranked in the top 10 of the listings – because 43% of people will only click the number one listing and more than 75% won't look beyond the first page of listings.[2]
5. An electronic marketer who understands e-marketing and how to sell other companies' products on your website.
6. A community relationship manager that knows how to get the most out of the traffic that can be generated from blogs, Twitter, Facebook, LinkedIn etc.

All of these elements working together will deliver a clearly focused website that:

- clarifies and 'anchors' what you offer by presenting the company and providing information.
- gets the phone to ring! Make it easy for prospects to get in touch – have telephone and contact details on every page.
- attracts buyers through free information, articles and give-aways. Most people (61%) are searching on the Internet for information. Being seen as the source of it and giving some away establishes you as an expert in your field in their minds.
- presents your products and services
- gives people a reason to return
- can be updated frequently
- is structured to build an opt-in list that will collect contact e-mail addresses and other contact details
- ranks highly enough in the search engines so that people who are looking for what you can do find you first (this is called 'search engine optimisation')
- tracks visitors and monitors the flow of traffic to see how long visitors stay on each page; this allows you to adjust the content to improve visitor retention.
- offers goods or services for sale on the site itself
- provides secure order-taking and banking with a clean and easy check-out process
- works with affiliates

Promoting your website

Although your website is a promotional tool for your business, it does need to be promoted itself for it to work effectively. One of the big challenges is getting visitors to the website in the first place. A variety of techniques are emerging to achieve this and you need to take a multi-threaded approach to be successful. Think of this as a second tier in your promotional efforts. The mix of possible approaches includes: use of key words and optimisation of the site in a way that excites the ranking engines; links to related sites; e-mail campaigns and so on.

Those, of course, are the basics. The ideal scenario is to make a website that is more like a 'destination attraction', somewhere that people want to go because it is attractive for them.

Think like a customer

The most important thing to remember about website design and related promotional tactics is that you must work out what your customers are thinking. What are they looking for? What needs are they trying to satisfy?

So many websites tell us about the business, what they do, describe products and so on. In the worst cases they simply act as an address card and frankly no-one cares! It's like putting a menu card outside a fish restaurant. It is irrelevant to most people; you are only going to look at it if you:

- **happen to notice it when passing**
- **are hungry**
- **fancy eating fish**
- **like the look of the place**
- **may be hungry for fish later, in which case you have to remember where the restaurant was**

As a way of building immediate or future business this is useless!

The Internet is a place where most people go for information. To retain the interest of anyone who has arrived at your home page, you need to be able to:

- offer easy navigation – less choice, not more
- answer the questions in your visitors' mind
- understand their needs
- know what is going to provoke the reaction 'found it!'
- provide reports and articles they are interested in
- think about product samples, free e-books and similar

The 1% problem

On average, less than 1% of people who visit a typical website take any action when they get there.[3] That means 99 out of 100 leave without doing anything or making contact with the owner.

For many websites, the figure is much lower than 1%. Do you know what the ratio of 'action visitors' to 'walk-aways' is for your site? This is a huge waste of money which should be fixed by making the site more 'sticky' for the target visitors.

How 'sticky' is your website? Most people will spend a maximum of eight seconds looking at a web page before moving on.[4] How can you grab people's attention, get them to stay with you and then dive deeper into whatever you are offering? Ask yourself:

- What are my visitors most interested in?
- What is the headline?
- Will whatever we have said on the first page hold their attention and encourage them to read on?
- Does the copy on our website communicate the specific benefits of what we can offer?
- Have we put as much free, useful information on the site as possible?
- Can we use more interesting ways to communicate and engage people, such as adding audio or video?

The purpose of your website

The key to getting the most value out of any investment in a website is to recognise the purpose of it. Since most people using the Internet are looking for information, use this as a key to unlock potential customers. Give them the information they're looking for in a useful, accessible way. This positions your business as a helpful expert, reduces 'engagement tension' (that is, any concerns they may have initially about working with a new supplier) and provides the rationale to open a path of communication which can then be used to build trust. Creating that communication pathway is what your website should be focused on. So the main purposes of your website are:

1. **as far as visitors are concerned, to provide useful information in an accessible way. Make sure that you get across the benefits of your products and services, not just product details**
2. **as far as your business is concerned, to collect the e-mail addresses of as many visitors as possible and gain their permission to use them. You'll then be able to communicate with them and build trust. When they're ready to buy, you want them to buy from *you*.**

So how do we collect these valuable addresses? It is no good just asking people to fill in a form; they won't do it if there is nothing in it for them. The first rule is to keep it quick and simple: you just want their e-mail address and name, rather than their family history. Secondly, provide an inducement: we know they have arrived at your home page for a reason, offer something that will work for your visitors in your market. An example might be

173

'Subscribe to our FREE Boosting Sales newsletter and we'll send you 10 tips guaranteed to increase your profits straight away'.

Use an auto-responder to send a confirmation as soon as people subscribe, then use the contact and name information they have provided to personalise your future communications.

The word 'personal' is important because people build relationships with other people, and you won't achieve it with the electronic version of leaflet drops or newspapers. So avoid the newsletter format, give something that adds value for them, which builds confidence and trust. As long as you are personal, relevant and useful, you'll start to build a relationship with these contacts. They'll begin to believe that you are great at what you do, many will convert to potential customers and ultimately become customers.

Persistence is key here. It takes constant contact over time to build confidence and trust.

E-mail

E-mail is, of course, a key part of Internet marketing and a massive subject in its own right. It's open to question whether e-mails are a promotional or a prospecting technique, since they are a form of communication that can be used as either. In truth, they fall into both camps.

Spam

E-mail is a promotional tool that can reach many people at the same time, just like any other form of advertising. But the indiscriminate 'carpet bombing' of large numbers of people with promotional messages – 'spamming' – doesn't work well. It is viewed negatively by both recipients and watchdogs alike. Avoid it *at all costs*.

The way to deal with the spam issue is easy; only send e-mails to people who have specifically agreed to receive them. Make sure your messages add value for your potential customers so that they will be pleased to receive them rather than groan at the sight of them in their inbox. Also make sure that you provide a simple mechanism for recipients to take themselves off your mailing list if they so wish.

Make it personal

The trick to prospecting with e-mails is to operate a sustained campaign that builds relationships by offering useful information. It is the giving away of useful nuggets (which does not, after all, cost you anything) that adds value for the recipient, positions you as an expert authority and creates a good impression. Think of yourself as a friend with a hot tip and adopt an appropriate style when you write: more relaxed than a letter, but not presumptuous.

Simple, personalised e-mails are best. Aim to get in touch with your customers and prospects at least twice a month.

Test different types of e-mails and different offers to see what works best for your customers. For example:

> Hi Sam,
>
> The long-range weather forecast is predicting a hot dry summer, so I am guessing that there will be a bumper fruit crop hitting your jam-making factory in the autumn.
>
> We have a new on-site repair service and I think this would be a good time to get your production line pumps checked over so that there is no down-time when production starts.
>
> I'll give you a call to talk about scheduling the work if that's okay. Any particular time suit you best?
>
> Best regards
>
> Jim Jones

Now imagine Sam as a hard-pressed production director, who probably didn't have time to even think of this issue earlier. Now he has the warning of a potential problem *and* the solution all in three paragraphs. No paper, no printing, no envelopes, no brochures, no stamps – how good is that? This is a shoestring technique if I ever saw one! You also have the benefit of being able to directly record what was sent and the response. This is direct response advertising of the purest kind because the response can be precisely related to the campaign.

So here we have a tool that:

- **communicates directly with potential customers**
- **costs nothing**
- **allows personal messages**
- **has global reach**
- **arrives within seconds**
- **provokes a prompt response**

The key to successful e-mail prospecting is to recognise that e-mail is a powerful communication tool in its own right. Make it stand out and use it to add value for your potential and existing customers while keeping them informed of your activities.

E-mail prospecting

Of course we can use a highly focused, targeted e-mail campaign to stimulate conversations with potential customers who might become actual customers. The first step is to collect the e-mail address of everyone who touches your business. Every time you do this you gain the opportunity to contact that person for free, as often you like, for as long as you like – until they tick the box saying they don't want any more.

One of the most useful ways of collecting e-mail addresses is through your website as previously mentioned. A thoughtful website design should provide an easy way for a visitor to submit their e-mail address and provide an inducement for doing so.

Once you know that people are happy for you to communicate with them, use this precious information effectively. Frankly, the types of businesses where e-mail can be used *directly* to sell things are very few. What you can do with e-mails is build confidence, trust and a relationship that will encourage people to purchase from you as soon as the benefit becomes obvious or the need arises.

Try:

- **thanking people for their interest**
- **thanking them for their business**
- **making a special offer**
- **giving away free information, such as an article or a report**
- **recommending a product or service they might be interested in**
- **asking for referrals**
- **sharing some news that is interesting to them**
- **asking why they haven't bought anything lately**

E-zines

I mentioned that the newsletter format doesn't work; this is because it lacks relevance, especially in the context of the personal communication and virtual relationship that we are endeavouring to create with our e-mail messages.

But outside of the 'make it personal' zone, an Internet newsletter, or e-zine – which is more like a magazine in that it contains articles with useful information – is a great way of regularly reminding people that you exist without the personal baggage. Provided it is published regularly – weekly, monthly or quarterly, say – it can do a number of things:

- **keep your name in the mind of potential customers**
- **help to establish you in their minds as an expert**
- **force you to package your knowledge concisely**

Think about developing an electronic newsletter of this type, but keep it as a separate thread from your relationship-building activities.

Notes/References

1. Furness F (2006). *www.frankfurness.com*
2. Gehl D (2006). *Marketing tips*, The Internet Marketing Centre, *www.marketing tips.com.*
3. Cardell, C. (2006). *www.cardellmedia.co.uk*
4. Cardell, C. (2006). *www.cardellmedia.co.uk.*

WORKING WITH OPPORTUNITIES

When all your prospecting and promotional activity starts to generate traffic, you need to think about qualifying these opportunities so that you can direct your selling efforts to those most likely to result in a sale.

An opportunity is anything that may lead us to a sale. But, to understand the nature of each one and how good it will be, requires further definition. We need to assess the amount, quality and context of the information we have to determine the likelihood of winning an order. This is called 'qualifying the opportunity'.

The first rule

When your promotional work results in an incoming enquiry, respond quickly: prospect interest generally only lasts for a limited time. So react promptly, be professional on the telephone and make it easy for them to buy from you.

But when we are flooded with opportunities (oh happy day!), it becomes important to describe our relationship with the people we are seeking to do, or are already doing, business with; in other words, qualify the relationship in terms of order potential.

Relationship status

A relationship can exist on many levels for example, a customer may also be a supplier, a source of leads to potential customers and a personal friend, for example. And a relationship can exist between people, departments and companies. This can make the single box you may have in your database or spreadsheet headed 'status' redundant.

I use two rules to help resolve this confusion:

1. **a relationship is always with a PERSON. There may be an affiliation with departments or companies, but it is always a PERSON who decides whether to buy. So you could have several customers within one company, which is good, but they will all have individual needs and ways of working and you must be able to meet those needs individually.**
2. **the relationship must be viewed from the sales perspective (because that is what we are trying to assess), and the highest potential value takes precedence in status-description terms. So the customer who is also a friend, supplier and source of leads is recorded as a customer because that describes his £ sales value to the organisation.**

Potential Population

Potential opportunities exist in any population we choose to look at which might turn into a source of business. They are probably vague ideas that will need further qualification to be of any value. For example, if we obtained a copy of the electoral roll for Scotland, we could research it to establish a list of potential people who might be interested in buying our thermal underwear this winter. So Scotland has a population with potential to buy, but we don't know enough about them to be able to sell them anything.

Suspects

A *suspect* has been identified as an opportunity but not yet contacted. Unlike *potentials*, suspects are not the population at large but that part of it which may want or need whatever it is that we supply. A big pool of suspects can be very good because we may have the opportunity to sell more. However, because we don't know much about them, it is hard to focus on their needs.

To qualify a potential as a suspect we need:

1. **gender**
2. **name**
3. **a way of communicating with them: a telephone number, e-mail or postal address**
4. **an indication of how likely they are to buy, in whatever way is meaningful for our business**

With this information to hand, we can at least get in touch with our suspect, with the objective of turning them into a *lead*, keeping them on the suspect list for later review or eliminating them altogether.

Leads

A *lead* is different from a potential population or a suspect in that we have more details about them. This enables us to make a personal and direct introduction of our products and services.

To qualify a lead we need to be sure that we are speaking to the right person and that there is a definite requirement for what we do either for them or their organisation.

But all leads are not equal . . .

Cold leads

A *cold* lead arises when we definitely know who we need to speak to and that they have a need for our products and services but there is no introduction, and no real way of gauging how our approach will be received.

Warm leads

A *warm* lead is when we have been introduced, which gives us a basis for an exploratory conversation to define the nature of the opportunity, and maybe engage interest and desire for what we do.

Hot leads

Hot leads are where the quality of the introduction or our previous activity has enabled us to identify the possibilty of working with the customer because we know we can supply what they need and they know that we can deliver. The challenge now is to turn that lead into a *prospect*.

Prospects

A prospect is someone we have contacted but who is not yet buying. Prospects differ from leads in that there is now a definite piece of business on the table to be discussed.

We therefore need more information, particularly when there are many factors influencing the buying process. But the key thing that distinguishes a prospect from a lead is when the opportunity is fully qualified or quoted:

Qualified prospects

For a prospect to be properly qualified we must have six key pieces of information.

1. **We know that there is a definite requirement and what is going to be required**
2. **We know where it has to be delivered to**
3. **We know or can estimate the budget**
4. **We are aware of the likely buying process the customer will operate, their buying tactics and how the negotiations will be conducted**
5. **We know the timescales for decision-making and delivery**
6. **Our contact has the authority and intention to purchase**

To illustrate, let's retreat a few years. You've been working on several leads all pointing to one job and have gathered information about several people who are involved in the decision-making, including the decision-maker. You now know that you are fit to meet the needs of the Millennium Dome Commission who are looking for someone to build the Mind Exhibit, in the Dome (Greenwich, London). They will be inviting tenders that will entail theatrical-style construction works to the order of the designer (the designs are still in progress) with an approximate value of £1,000,000. Everyone knows that it has to be completed for 31 December 1999 for the millennium celebrations, contracts will be let on 31 March 1999, so they will be looking to receive tender responses by early February that year.

The matrix of strengths, weaknesses, opportunities and threats with which your organisation operates will define your appetite for this opportunity – but that is a qualified prospect. Go for it if you dare!

Quoted prospects

If we are about to offer a price for our goods and services or make a quotation, this is where things start to get really serious.

By now we will have invested a considerable amount of time, effort and maybe money in getting the opportunity properly qualified.

For a quoted prospect, we should have added to the six qualifying keys to build up an Intelligence Jigsaw[1] that forms a 'picture' of the prospect to the extent that, even if one or two pieces are missing, we can still get an idea of the whole image. The idea is to learn enough about the potential customer that we can 'pitch' our offer in such a way that it stands the best chance of acceptance.

This Intelligence Jigsaw will include as many of these components as possible:

1. **Background information on the prospect company**
2. **A description of the decision-making process**
3. **An organisation chart that includes the people we are dealing with**
4. **A list of the key people involved with the decision making. We need to know:**

   a) **their positions in the organisation**
   b) **their degree of influence on the decision**
   c) **whether they are 'for us' or 'against us'**
   d) **as much other information we can accumulate that will help to foster a positive relationship.**

5. **An understanding of their objectives and where we can add value with our proposition**
6. **The total amount of the type of goods and/ or services we are offering that the prospect buys in any given period and how much of this business we share with any competitors that may also be supplying them**

7. An understanding of the strength of our position and how vulnerable we might be to competitor activities if they try and win more of our business from this customer

We now have to invest more time in costing the work, deciding the price and adding all the other supplementary information that will help the customer understand that we are the best firm to give his patronage to.

It's so important to properly qualify the opportunity before we get to this stage because, for complex proposals, it may take several weeks and cost money to put an acceptable offer together.

Order likelihood

Having an idea of how likely it is that you'll win an order is highly important. A lot of effort, time and money has been invested in getting a potential customer far enough into the sales process so that an offer can be tendered. Understanding the 'hit' rate is critical to the shoestring approach of only spending money where we have the best likelihood of a return.

Also, the value of any business entity is directly related to its sales potential and the profit that will generate. Whenever a business goes up for sale, potential buyers will closely analyse the prospects and how likely those orders are likely to materialise.

In addition:

1. It is essential to estimating and planning the cash and other resources that will be required to fulfil the orders we actually win.

2. The amount of work you have coming in is a critical indicator of the future security of the business.

Because estimating this order likelihood is so important, we need some kind of system for assessing it. Sales people are always optimistic, so just asking them may not give a sufficiently accurate answer. Even if *you* are doing the selling in your business, you need a rationale. Deriving this estimate depends upon the answers to these questions:

1. **Do we understand the sales process for this opportunity and how far are we into it?**
2. **Have we offered a price?**

Sales process

Sales processes can be very simple, such as a spontaneous purchase where someone just calls and orders something for immediate delivery.

Many firms have an element of 'bluebird' business (it just flew in and surprised us) or regular small orders such as 'We always sell £8,000 of spare parts each month'.

Provided this business is regular and small (say less than 10% of the sales volume), then I would just put it on the opportunities-tracking schedule as a single line. I'd also want to figure out how we can get more of it at some point, so it is important not to lose sight of it!

They can also have a limited number of definable stages such as an enquiry, quotation, order cycle:

- **enquiry received**
- **prospect qualified**
- **needs assessed**
- **quotation offered**
- **negotiations progressing**
- **commitment to buy**

Alternatively, they can be very complex, such as a competitively tendered construction project.

If you have a number of partially qualified opportunities and can at least hazard a guess about the probable order value, you might estimate that (say) 5% of these will result in an order eventually. The actual percentage success rate will be specific to the sector your business operates in and the success of your sales activities. However, a good safe rule is to assume that no-one ever persuaded anyone to buy anything without offering a price. Therefore, if no price has been offered, no quotation raised or no bid tendered, it's unlikely you'll get an order.

Price and likelihood

Once an offer has been made, what do we feel about the chances of acceptance? This depends upon the quality of the opportunity, which is informed by the qualifying criteria (otherwise we wouldn't have got this far in the first place), as well as some other things:

1. We have a way of understanding the likely budget and our offer is within it
2. We know the timescales for decision-making and delivery as well as the customer's decision-making process and can meet them
3. We know that there is a definite requirement, the scope of supply, where it is and we and our prospects are comfortable with our ability to meet their requirements
4. We understand the quality of our relationship with the decision-maker who has the authority and intention to purchase and also understand who the other

    **influencers of the decision are and our relationships
with them**

5. **Previous quotation and trading history**
6. **Competitor activity**

It is essential to be clear and consistent about the criteria for
judgement in the first place. Subsequently, keeping a record of
achievements will help increase accuracy.

Here are some examples of opportunities from a branch of the
construction industry and how the likelihood of winning an order
from them might be expressed.

Unfancied

'We've offered quotations to this contractor, six times in the past,
our last four prices were always within budget but we have never
won an order. Why not? Do we stand any chance of ever winning
an order from them?'

I'd imagine that the likelihood of winning an order from that
opportunity is **0%** until we've had chance to find out we weren't
being given an even chance.

Nothing special

'Our tender has been submitted for the fit-out works and we're pre-
qualified to do the work. We have no special relationship with the
buyers, though, and six of us are up for the job.' No better than
10% (to stand any chance at all, we'd have to get their attention
with a competitive price).

Negotiable affection

'It's down to the last two or three, so we are in with a great chance
and I think they will want to negotiate directly with us.' **20%** (it's

never an even chance across the competitors because they are all just as determined to win as you are and the customer will use this as a bargaining tool.

Last dance

'I'm sure we're going to win this. Ours is the best price, the best specification, I played golf with the buyer last Saturday and he told me our competitor doesn't stand a chance.' **50%** (he plays golf with the competitor as well – the one who has the last dance often gets to go home with the girl, but it's never certain!)

Dating

'We have an enabling contract with this customer, provided we quote according to the agreed schedule of rates, we are always awarded the work.' **80%** (only because you are not in control of all the circumstances governing the award, so don't mess it up!)

Engaged

'We've been jumped through all the hoops the customer's set out for us. We have a great relationship and he's promised us the order.' **90%** (about one in ten of these falls over for some reason outside your control).

Influencers

Influencers are not opportunities because they themselves are unlikely to buy. Nevertheless, it's important to recognise the key role they play in the buyer's decision-making process and the effect they have on order likelihood. Influencers can include:

- **'gatekeepers': receptionists, secretaries and personal assistants**

- **consultants**
- **referrers**
- **competitors: these can be classified according to their capacity to interfere and so can be 'cold', 'warm' or 'hot'**
- **suppliers: contractors, distributors, manufacturers, resellers, retailers, vendors wholesalers and so on**
- **network contacts: family, friends, employees, co-workers, investors, shareholders, accounts, bankers and so on**

Of course, with a complex sale there may be many influencers *inside* the customer's organisation affecting the buying decision. This can be a useful tool for mapping the influencers of a sale:[2]

		Hardly Influences				Decision Maker
		A	B	C	D	E
Will Recommend Us	1					
	2					
	3					
	4					
Will Recommend Competition	5					

Figure 12.1

Next time you have a complex sale, try putting the names of the influencers in the relevant boxes. What can you do to move everyone involved to the top right-hand corner?

The main thing to remember about influencers is that they do exist and you have to manage them so that their input on the buyer's decision-making is weighted in your favour.

Eliminating opportunities

Many of the prospecting techniques described are going to produce traffic – a lot of it if you are taking the recommended multi-thread approach. But you can't win them all and not all opportunities are worth pursuing. When it comes to eliminating opportunities, there are two schools of thought.

Many of the prospecting techniques described are going to produce traffic – a lot of it if you are taking the recommended multi-thread approach. But you can't win them all and not all opportunities are worth pursuing. When it comes to eliminating opportunities, there are two schools of thought.

The first is that 'persistence pays'. This approach *is* valid but only if you have multiple business opportunities that are allowing you to hit your target numbers anyway and only a small proportion of your time is spent on shaking trees that may never bear fruit. The second approach is that giving up on a lost cause sets you free to go and look for more likely opportunities.

Both approaches are right when sensibly balanced but not at the extremes. Many an unsuccessful sales person has been asked to hand back their car keys when they spent too much time flogging a 'dead' contact list and didn't look elsewhere.

Don't be lazy and look only for easy targets, because everyone else is looking for those too and you will be forced to compete for them.

There is another type of opportunity to be watchful for. That is the customer who always welcomes your approach, then takes up large amounts of your time 'pumping' you for information but never actually buys anything. The way to avoid this trap is by diligently qualifying the opportunity as described above.

Notes/References

1. Jesson, P. (2004). Business Pulse & Pareto, www.theparetopartnership.com & *www.philjesson.com*
2. Jesson, P. (2004). Business Pulse & Pareto, www.theparetopartnership.com.

13 TRACKING AND CLOSING

What is it that's actually going to bring about the growth we aspire to? The answer is that *measuring* things makes them happen. Here, we'll look at a number of tracking tools that will help you make sure your sales-boosting activities are as effective as possible.

Some way of tracking the effectiveness of our selling activities – such as recording the generation and qualification of suspects, leads and prospects – is essential and there are many mechanisms to help you do that. They can range from simple card index systems, to computerised address books such as Microsoft Outlook, contact management systems such as ACT! or GoldMine®, or even fully-blown customer relationship management (CRM) systems that integrate with the accounting and other business functions.

Simple is best. The problem with elaborate, high-end systems is that they are expensive and difficult to set up, which is not the shoestring way at all. Furthermore, even in relatively small organisations there are real difficulties in getting everyone to be motivated, consistent and accurate about putting information into the system.

Whichever system you choose to use, the basic information we need to capture is driven by what we are trying to measure and control. I'll describe here the type of data we need to acquire and how we use it to powerfully drive the business forward.

Why? Why? Why?

One of the best ways of discovering what is likely to generate new business is to get to the root of what causes sales.

This can be different for every business and sometimes needs some discussion with the sales team, but understanding what actually results in new orders is key for planning your cost-effective sales-boosting activities. One way is to keep asking *why* something happened until you get to the action that led to an order. For example:

- **Why did the customer buy?** *She liked our offer.*
- **Why did we make an offer?** *She needed what we do.*
- **Why did he need what we do?** *We qualified the prospect to find out what she wanted*
- **Why did we find a prospect?** *We had a lead.*
- **Why did we get a lead?** *We went to a networking event.*

And so on. There will of course be several ways in which leads are being generated because we are using a multi-thread approach to prospecting and promoting. This leads us into the concept of the 'sales funnel'.

The sales funnel

The sales funnel is a way of describing the way that opportunities are channelled from potential 'clouds of opportunity' into becoming suspects, then leads, into prospects and eventually orders. While some orders can happen by chance, the sales funnel recognises that there is a process involved in building a reliably consistent stream of business, which can look like this:

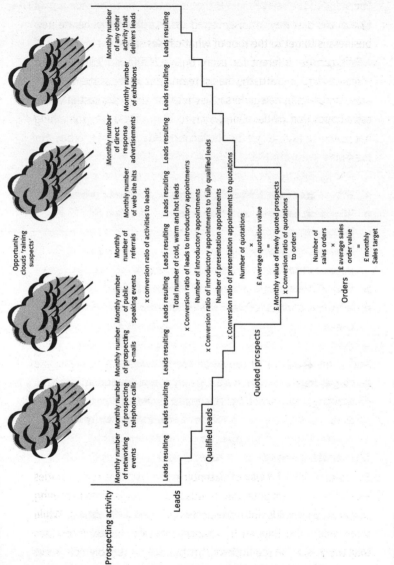

Figure 13.1

The value of the sales funnel is that it enables us to provide a plan of our sales activities in a way that helps us quantify the results. You may remember that the number of new orders required by Jones Ltd was 25 jobs for a total gross profit of £402,500 and 5,750 hours.

Notice that I'm not using the traditional measures of turnover and gross margin percentage because these are irrelevant to the value-added approach we are taking.

- If our annual sales target is £402,500 of gross profit and 5,750 hours of man/machine hours over 25 jobs, this represents £33,542 of gross profit per month and 480 hours across about two jobs.
- If the conversion ratio of quotations to orders in that business is one in four, then they need to be raising eight quotations per month (2 × 4), or about one every two to three days. These are the *quoted prospects*.
- If one in every five presentation meetings results in a request for a quotation, the sales team should be making 50 presentation appointments per month (2 × 4 × 5). These are the *qualified prospects*.
- If one in every four leads results in a presentation meeting, we need 160 leads per month (2 × 4 × 5 × 4).
- If one in ten suspects we communicate with results in a lead, then our prospecting and promotional activities need to be addressing a suspect pool of around 1,600 opportunities.

Of course, different types of businesses will have different conversion ratios and these will vary according to the industry and the effectiveness of the promotional activity. But for this example we've now established that it will take 50 customer appointments to achieve our sales target. If there are 20 working days in the month and a reasonable sales person can do one appointment a day (because of the geography of the appointments, difficulty of real-world scheduling and the need to take time out for quotations and prospecting), Jones Ltd is going to need three good sales people.

Achieving 160 leads a month has important implications for the prospecting activity. However, the multi-thread approach may mean that the idea of a single sales funnel is too simplistic. Inevitably, the number of personal prospecting activities such as networking or speaking events may be quite small because of the time they soak up, but it could be that these produce very high-quality leads with a much higher conversion ratio than that assumed by our sales funnel. Referrals should produce warm or hot leads that are relatively easy to convert to orders. On the other hand, the order conversion ratios for e-mails and website hits may be much worse, but the good news is that it costs little in time or money to generate these.

What we need to do is look at each prospecting activity that we have decided to use in isolation and imagine what its sales funnel progress would be. We then have to estimate the prospecting-hits-to-order-conversion rate for that activity. If we make a note of our original estimates and then compare them, eventually, with the actual results, we'll arrive at the prospecting cost per order of each of our different types of prospecting activity. This is absolutely crucial to the success of our sales-boosting campaign, because inevitably some of our prospecting tools are going to be more cost-effective than others, and we need to be focusing on the ones that work best for us.

This doesn't mean that we're aiming to reduce our prospecting to the one most efficient technique eventually, because the whole point of the multi-thread approach is that different customers need to be reached in different ways. What we *are* seeking to do is eliminate those activities that are completely unproductive and limit the money we spend on those techniques which work don't work as well but bring in valuable customers nonetheless.

Here's an example of a partially completed monthly prospecting activity record:

Monthly prospecting activity record	Networking events	Telephone calls	E-mails	Public speaking	Referrals	Web site hits	Direct response ads	Exhibitions
Money cost £	£ 100	£ 24						
Time cost (hours)	6	20						
Number	2	240						
Leads	8	12						
Introductory appt	63							
Qualified leads	5	1						
Presentation appt	41							
Quoted prospects	4	1						
Number of orders	2	1						
Value of orders	£ 20,000	£ 10,000						

Figure 13.2

Note that in addition to the monetary cost of each activity, the time cost in hours is also recorded. This is extremely important for a small business, because the amount of time that key people will have to devote to these activities can be limited. If you have to spend 16 hours preparing for, and then delivering at a public speaking event, you definitely need to know how many orders resulted from it!

Prospecting campaigns

Once we have refined the sales funnel concept into an individual funnel for each activity, we can more precisely understand the value of each prospecting technique if we further divide them into prospecting campaigns.

A prospecting campaign may consist of a single activity bound by time or a group of activities all targeted at a particular customer group or sector.

The idea is that a prospecting event may be defined by a number of parameters that will enable us to set a budget, control it and measure the results in a particular period.

A campaign definition for a small dinghy manufacturer planning to 'hit' a boat show might look like this:

Boat Show Campaign	Networking Events	Direct Response Ads	Exhibitions	Totals
Start date: 20th Sept 2007				End date: 25th Sept 2007
Money cost £	£ 500	£ 5,000	£ 20,000	£ 25,500
Time cost (hours)	8	25	80	113
Number	2	1	1	
Suspects	240	12000	8000	20240
Leads	60	150	400	610
Introductory appt	60	20	70	
Qualified leads	60	12	60	
Presentation appt	35	10	40	
Quoted prospects	30	6	35	
Number of orders	2	2	8	12
Value of orders	£ 100,000	£ 20,000	£ 80,000	£ 200,000

Figure 13.3

In this example, the exhibition costs were £20,000 and 80 hours were spent in setting up, manning the stand and then dismantling it. Out of the 8,000 people who attended the show 400 people visited the stand, which subsequently resulted in 8 orders for little boats. In parallel with this an advertisement was placed in a yachting magazine with 12,000 subscribers, and because of the special offer code attached to the advertisement we know that this resulted in 2 sales. Finally, there were lots of evening parties at the show and we attended two of them, recording them on our 'expenses' claim as networking events, which was OK because we sold ten boats as a result.

So total direct costs (excluding employee time costs that are included in business overheads) were £25,500 and 113 hours for £200,000 of sales. If the gross margin on these sales was 25%, earning a £50,000 contribution, then the campaign covered its costs (but you'd have to wonder whether the effort was worth it in this case!).

Value of the business stream

The value of the business stream can be estimated with two lists. The first is simply a schedule of the leads and qualified prospects, so we can keep track of opportunities that are at these stages of the sales funnel. What we are interested in here is whether we have sufficient opportunities in each category of relationship that the business needs. No monetary value is attributable because no price has been established yet.

The second list details the qualified and quoted prospects and assigns a 'business-stream value' by multiplying the value of the gross profit derived from the quotation by the 'prospect likelihood'. You will know the gross margin and the amount of profit that is likely to result because you costed the job and then decided on the price to offer it to the customer. You will also know the second figure from the 'quoted prospect likelihood' percentages you worked out for your own business from the examples above.

The other really useful detail to have in this table is the number of resource hours the job will consume, weighted in the same way.

Although these lists could obviously be combined, it is better to keep them separate because the distinction between unqualified and qualified opportunities means they each need a different selling focus. Separating them you get the best possible feel for two essential criteria:

■ whether the business is likely to be able to earn enough money to sustain it
■ whether it is likely to be able to cope with the workload required to earn it

See opposite for some business-stream tables.

List 1 - Suspects and Leads:

Sales Person	Customer Name	Opportunity Name	Job Type	Likely Order Date	Qualifier	Source of Opportunity
RDG	Acme Foods Ltd	Summer refit	Pumps service	May-07	Relationship status such as: • Suspect • Cold lead • Warm lead • Hot lead	Whatever brought the opportunity to our attention, such as: • The prospecting campaign • A list we obtained • A referer • Or similar

List continues to schedule as many opportunities as you can see

List 2 - Prospects

Sales Person	Customer Name	Opportunity Name	Job Type	Likely Order Date	Qualifier	Source of Opportunity	Likely Order Value	Likely Gross Profit	Est Labour Hours	Value Added per Hour	Likelihood
RDG	Smith Ltd	London plant	New pumps	Sep-07	Relationship status such as: • Qualified prospect • Quoted prospect	Whatever brought the opportunity to our attention, such as: • The prospecting campaign • A list we obtained • A referer • Or similar	£ 5,000	£ 1,500	16	£ 93.75	50%
RDG	Jones Ltd	Kent factory	Pump repair	Apr-07	Relationship status such as: • Qualified prospect • Quoted prospect	Whatever brought the opportunity to our attention, such as: • The prospecting campaign • A list we obtained • A referer • Or similar	£ 10,000	£ 4,000	50	£ 80.00	80%

List continues to schedule as many prospects as you can see
Then summarise the business stream total by multiplying each value
by the likelihood and adding them together thus:

Estimated value of business stream: £ 13,500 | £ 3,950 | 48 | £ 82.29

Figure 13.4

For clarity, I've shown the minimum amount of information you should be tracking. You can, of course, add as much other detail as you like (like competitors, for example), but one golden rule is to keep the tables as simple as possible so that they're easy to maintain. However, one really useful column is the 'value added' one: this shows, at a glance, which prospects are the best ones for the business! A useful predictor of future fortune, don't you think?

Closing the sale

There is a classic and well known model for describing the stages that lead to a sale and it is described by the acronym AIDA. This stands for:

- **Attention – engaging the attention of the prospective customer to look at your offer**
- **Interest – exciting their interest in the proposal**
- **Desire – creating a wish to purchase**
- **Action – moving them to buy**

Once the 'elevator pitch' has done its work of getting attention and interest, you need to move the customer on to the next two stages of the model. This means creating their desire to buy the product or service and then closing the deal.

The professional approach to winning orders is to spend time establishing a rapport, then investigating the customer's needs. The technique is to sell yourself by showing interest in the other person (because people buy from people), and then ask the right questions.

This is called *consultative selling* and there are seven stages to closing a sale which have to be worked through in a certain order. Each stage requires a different amount of time to be devoted it, as indicated below:

Selling activity	Proportion of time devoted to the activity			
	1	2	3	4
1	Find common ground, get accepted and build a trusting relationship			
2	Opening statement and qualify by establishing needs, desires and budget			
3	Ask questions and get information (don't sell)			
4	Check assumptions and relate them to earlier questions			
5	Match the offer to what has been learned – this is the main pitch and time to reveal your unique selling proposition			
6	Double check that the offer meets the needs			
7	Close the sale at the appropriate point			

Figure 13.5

One small point: a consultative selling approach does not mean that you should allow yourself to be dragged into a morass of technical details. Effective selling relies on empathy and trust more than it does on specifications. Although a balance of product and industry knowledge is required, too much technical detail is unnecessary to building a relationship and should be delegated to the 'experts'. Remember that people buy emotionally and justify intellectually.

Throughout this process, remember that customers will still be buying what your product or service does for them, so keep everything focused on the benefits to them. And don't forget to ask for the order!

12 point checklist for boosting sales on a shoestring

1. Make sure you really do want to boost sales and then define where you are going with a one page business plan.
2. Work out:

- your current trading condition
- self financing growth rate (cash)
- critical resource limitation
- break-even value added point
- target value added point

3. Identify your most *profitable* customers and grow business with them first.
4. Use 'dynamic pricing' to maximise profitability through making the best use of the resources available to you.
5. Improve your business's efficiency.
6. Identify and target the right customers to retain.
7. Accept the competition for what it is and play to your strengths.
8. Create a 'sticky' identity for your business.
9. Set out to find the right type of new customers with a multi-threaded approach using 8 to 10:

   - Prospecting campaigns
   - Promotional campaigns
   - Online (both)

10. Qualify opportunities and reach for the 'low hanging fruit'.
11. Monitor and track all prospecting campaigns, promotions, opportunities and sales so that you get maximum return on your efforts.
12. Close the sale!

Notes/ References

1 Kramer, K. (2001). *CEO Tools*, Gandy Dancer Press.

INDEX